TIME & PLACE

The Path provided for Bill Humphrey, a Hall of Fame Umpire

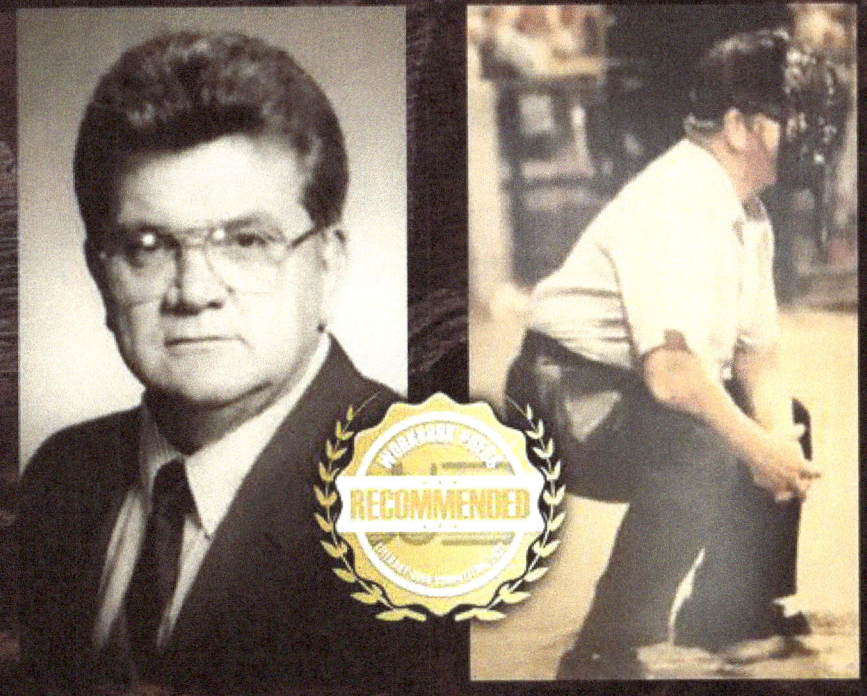

RECOMMENDED

David Schimpf

WORKBOOK PRESS LLC

187 E Warm Springs Rd,

Suite B285, Las Vegas, NV 89119, USA

Website:https://workbookpress.com/

Hotline:1-888-818-4856

Email:admin@workbookpress.com

Ordering Information:

Quantity sales. Special discounts are available on quantity purchases by corporations, associations, and others.

For details, contact the publisher at the address above.

Library of Congress Control Number:

ISBN-13:   978-1-960752-61-1 (Paperback Version)

             978-1-960752-62-8 (Digital Version)

REV. DATE: 02/02/2023

FOREWORD

How does one tell the story of a legend? That was the task before me once I asked for permission from Bill Humphrey and he agreed, to put his life story in a book and have it published.

I approached Bill about this back in the summer of 2021 while we were watching a fast pitch softball game. He was taken back by the request and it took some convincing to get him to agree that it was so important to get his achievements, past stories, and thoughts in writing.

Bill knew about the book I had written, **"From Boys to Men"** about my years in the military, especially Vietnam, and he said he was impressed. During the Covid pandemic of 2020, I finished this and had it published. This obviously helped "sell" the idea of writing about his life.

When I say Bill Humphrey is a legend, it is not an exaggeration. Bill was, and is, an absolute icon in the softball world. Few, if any, have dedicated their lives to such an organization as the Amateur Softball Association (ASA), now known as the USA Softball of America Organization. His knowledge, insight, perception, and ideas helped place softball as one of the premier recreational sports in the United States and the world.

Now Bill is a humble man. More humble than many believe. He immediately said he really didn't want a book about him but more about the great game of softball. He said many times that without softball and ASA he would be nothing. He continually praised the game, ASA and the Michigan Amateur Softball Association (MASA) whenever we talked.

I couldn't agree more with him as I know my career as an umpire would not have been what it was without the great game and ASA and MASA. I always wanted to write a book about softball and this was also a great means to tell that history of the game.

I interviewed Bill numerous times either in his beautiful back yard in Midland, Michigan, or various restaurants in the area. I quickly realized this was no easy task. Bill loves to talk softball. Even at age 83, his memory remains razor sharp. I love to listen to his many stories.

Breakfast would quickly become lunch or even dinner time. Usually it would end with strawberry shortcake and two scoops of "Dolly Parton" ice cream. I would always have to warn the waitress about the meaning of that before the request was made. I won't go into great detail but he would reverse his two hands facing his chest and......well......you figure the rest out. No waitress ever took offense, just laughter, and then the result was one great dessert.

Before long I had plenty of notes and details to put together a start of telling Bill's story. I decided it would be a "two part" book, which would tell the history of the game of softball and lead into the second part, Bill's story. Afterall, Bill stated the importance of softball many, many times. How appropriate to tell that story as well.

Most historians will attest that the game of softball began in the fall of 1887 in Chicago simply by accident. A group of young men, graduates of either Harvard or Yale were at the Farragut Boat Club listening the results of the Harvard vs Yale football game taking place in New England. George W. Hancock manufactured a ball quickly, a broom stick, and the rest is history. The entire story is told in "Part One" of this book.

As I poured myself over researching I became enamored over how softball evolved. The photos, articles, and statistics were amazing. Because the game was spread early on over decades and difficult times, I decided it was important to include those details in the book as well. The late 1800's as the game quickly grew, then World War I would occur, followed by the great depression of the 30's and then World War II. All would play a huge part in the game and I felt this also had to be told.

Finding information about the game proved far easier than obtaining and putting together the life story of Bill Humphrey. I wanted to do it my way, but I also wanted to gain the respect from Bill by doing it "right". No easy task. Anyone who truly knows Bill realizes this. He gave me full rights to do whatever I wanted as long as I always gave credit to all of those people who were so much a part of softball and his life. The list of people Bill thinks highly of is enormous. He rarely left anyone out. I would try to include as many as humanly possible.

Achieving great goals during the decades of the 1960's to 1970's as an umpire was not easy. Especially if you were a fast pitch umpire, like Bill. There was the Men's Major and Women's Major Fast Pitch along with the Men's Major and Women's Major slow pitch. That was it. Unlike the 21st century when Junior Olympic (J.O.) national tournaments, modified pitch and numerous slow pitch would explode across the country.

It was slim pickings for an umpire during Bill's prime, but he basically achieved his goals. He was one of the premier umpires in the country and word quickly spread about his ability to umpire.

Without going into great detail here, I will let you read his story in "Part Two". A young teenage baseball player who would rise through the softball umpire ranks, become a state (Michigan) and national Umpire-in-Chief, Commissioner, and eventually president of ASA. His leadership and foresight would grow the umpire program into arguably the best in the nation.

His achievements and accolades are second to none as far as I am concerned. He is in the ASA national Hall of Fame, as well as Michigan and other state Hall of Fames. Many awards in his lifetime and awards named in his honor.

The next task was to find the appropriate title. This would be not as difficult as I thought. Many times Bill would say his career evolved because of time and place. I decided to select that as a title and ran it by Bill for his "stamp of approval". He was elated. So that's how "**Time & Place**" came to be.

Again, Bill Humphrey is much too humble, and would probably not want all this praise, but it is well deserved. I just hope I didn't do any disservice telling his story so we both can be proud.

Now, sit back, enjoy the story of the great game of softball and the story of a great umpire and man, dedicated to the "Game"!

Chapter One
The Origin of Softball

In order to tell the Bill Humphrey story, the game of softball has to be included. This chapter will tell the actual beginning of the great game we all know and love.

There are many who believe the game of softball is just a variant of baseball and just as many say, "no, the game of softball was invented in a gymnasium by a bunch of young men wanting a good time." Unlike Baseball or basketball, the actual inventor is basically unknown as is the original location of the game. So, perhaps it is just a variation of the game of baseball and there never actually was a time and place of its origin.

The printed volume of the Indoor Baseball Guide of 1906, published by the American Sports Publishing Company recognizes the following: "The origin of the game of softball or indoor baseball is credited with Mr. George W. Hancock of the Farragut Boat Club* in Chicago." Just as amazing is the fact that the game of football played a huge part in it.

Yale was playing Harvard in one of the greatest football rivalries on a brisk, cold Thanksgiving Day, November 24th, in 1887. Members of the Farragut Boat Club met in Chicago to get updates on the game by way of the telegraph and news came that Yale had defeated Harvard 17-8, a Yale enthusiast picked up an old boxing glove and threw it at a nearby Harvard alum. He promptly tried to hit it back with a stick as George Hancock, a reporter for the Chicago Board of Trade, watched in amusement.

Suddenly George shouted out, "Let's play ball!" The boys hauled out a huge wrestling mat as George tied the boxing glove into the shape of a ball. The broken broom handle was used as a bat and before long the boys drew a large diamond with chalk. This proved to be great fun and as George watched the boys playing he thought of a plan to play an organized game.

He called the boys together an as they surrounded him he told them of his game plan and a few rules on how to play. He then said, "I believe this affair can be worked into a regular game of baseball which can be played indoors, and if you all come down Saturday night I'll make up some rules and have a ball and bat which will suit the purpose of the sport and do no damage to the surroundings."

So, on Saturday night, twenty boys showed up and two teams were chosen, George read the rules he made up and presented the teams with a huge ball and small rubber-tipped bat which has since been identified with the game of softball. The game began and before long it was obvious that great fun was being had by all. Members and spectators went away with loud praises at what they just witnessed and before long the game was being played all around the city.

Although all twenty boys who played that Saturday is not known, these were present along with George Hancock. It is presumed these were also part of the original players during the Thanksgiving game.

Frank Staples, 162 30th Street, Chicago, a cashier.

Tom Jenkins, 243 Monroe street, dry goods merchant.

Al Porter, 3116 Forest Avenue, shipping merchant.

Ogden Downs, 235 Michigan Avenue, salesman.

Warren Kniskern, 3245 Vernon Avenue, passenger agent for Northwestern Railway.

August White, 3842 Johnson Place, commission merchant.

Lyman B. Glover, 3041 Groveland Avenue, theater manager.

Carl Bryant, 3228 Groveland Avenue, bookkeeper.

Edwin Anderson, Farragut Boat Club, superintendent.

Edward Palmer, 629 43rd Street, watchman.

The game became very popular in Chicago during the winter of 1887 when indoor softball could be played in many gymnasiums. The Farragut Boat Club team challenged and played numerous teams from other clubs and sections of the city. During springtime, it was played in any sizable room with dimensions allowing for proper bases. Because many large rooms weren't always the same size, base distances and pitching distances varied.

Hancock then decided to sit down and write out specific rules and regulations in order to have some resemblance to uniformity. He wrote the game should be played like ordinary baseball with regulations to equalize the difference in size of the grounds and surroundings. The ball should be 16" in circumference, made of a yielding substance. The bat is 2 feet, 9 inches long and 1 and a ¼ inches in diameter at the large end. Each base shall be 18" square and filled with sand. Thus the name "bag" became the normal nomenclature.

The catcher should always play up close to the batter as foul tips are frequent, and the composition of the ball won't cause serious injury if he got hit or struck in the face. Hancock then wrote nineteen special rules which he felt necessary for use indoors, especially when abreviated spaces were necessary. These rules were officially adopted by the Mid-Winter Indoor Baseball League of Chicago on October 24, 1889 and read as follows:

1. The Pitcher's box shall be 6 by 3 feet to be marked on the floor; the nearest line of said box to be 22 feet from home base. This distance is not to be varied.
2. The bases to be 27 feet from each other, forming a diamond, where the size of the hall will allow. Should the hall be too narrow, the distance between first and third bases may be lessened.

3. The distance from home to second base should always be 37 ½ feet.

4. Nine or eight men may be played on each side.

5. Only shoes with rubber soles may be worn.

6. Only straight-armed pitching, in which the arm and hand swing parallel with the body will be allowed, and the ball is not to be curved.

6. A batted ball which falls inside or on the foul line is fair, the first point of contact with the floor, object or player, deciding, regardless of where it afterwards rolls.

7. A batted ball first striking outside the foul lines shall be foul.

8. The third strike caught before touching the ground is out.

9. A foul tip or foul fly caught before touching the ground is out.

10. Four unfair pitched balls give the batsman first base.

11. A pitched ball striking the batter is a dead ball, but does not entitle him to a base. If it should be the third strike, the batter is out, and no base shall be run on the ball.

12. A base runner must not leave his base on a pitched ball not struck, until after it has reached or passed the catcher on penalty of being called back.

13. A base runner must not leave his base while the pitcher holds the ball standing in his box.

14. A batted ball, caught after striking any wall, or fixture, shall be considered first bound, and is not out.

15. In over-running first base the runner can turn either way

in returning.

16. If a batter intentionally kicks or interferes with a ball he has just batted, he is out.

17. If a batted ball, after striking fair, rebounds and hits the batter, he shall not be declared out because of this.

18. The game shall be judged by two umpires: one shall take a position in center field and give decisions on second and third base plays, and shall see that a base runner does not leave any base before a pitched ball has reached the catcher. The other umpire shall take a position behind the catcher and judge all other points of the game. The two umpires shall change positions at the end of every inning. Umpires shall not be chosen from the two clubs contesting.

To dispel any doubt regarding Chicago's claim to the birthplace of softball, The following documentation is presented: "An amusement which is purely Chicagoan, invented by a Chicagoan, and little known outside the city limits is 'indoor baseball.' The game was invented in 1887 by George W. Hancock, of the Farragut Club, and has now become a recognized and leading feature among winter diversions. It is played in any hall large enough for the purpose with a miniature diamond marked in chalk, a soft ball, and a light bat."

By the summer of 1887, there was about 100 organized indoor ball clubs in Chicago, and their games attracted thousands of spectators. Indoor baseball became a sport of gentlemen, and most importantly, club members. These clubs became very prominent in the city, besides numerous independent organizations in the city and suburbs. The two leading leagues in Chicago were the "Midwinter" and "Chicago Indoor Base Ball League." The strongest teams were the Kenwoods, LaSalles, Oaks of Austin, Idlewilds of Evanston, Carletons, Marquettes, Farraguts, and Ashlands of the Midwinter League. The Indoor League had the Harvards, Lincoln Cycling Club, Chicago Cycling Club and South Side Illinois Club.

It didn't take long before the sport was being played outdoors in playgrounds, fields, and baseball diamonds but on a smaller scale. It is here that the origin of the name evolved into "Indoor – Outdoor", as it was called in many sections of the country.

As the game quickly was catching on in America and even Canada and before the year ended the premier publication of the "Indoor Baseball Guide" occurred. This was the first nationally distributed publication on the new game and it lasted in popularity internationally with a formation of an actual league in Toronto, Canada.

In the spring of 1888, the mass appeal of the game forced it mainly outdoors played on a small diamond. It also had many other names, such as: Kittenball, Mushball, and even Pumpkinball. By the summer of that year, other states such as Minnesota and Iowa were quickly forming leagues. Playground leaders in Minneapolis and St. Paul saw the possible growth of this game and soon worked out a code of rules which became the basic framework of the rules used today.

The first woman's game of softball is known to begin in 1895. It could have begun sooner than that but no known history has been verified. That game became the standard form of what eventually became women's baseball also.

The Minneapolis Story

Minneapolis became the next large metropolis to promote and foster this new game of "Indoor baseball". From its beginning in 1895 the city of Minneapolis played a major part in the expansion of this fast growing popular sport. The game began in Minneapolis by Lewis Rober Sr, then the Lieutenant of Minneapolis Fire Company No. 11. Because communication was so slow during these years it is not known for certain if Lieutenant Rober had heard of the game being played in Chicago. It is perceived that Rober conceived of the game in the same manner as George Hancock.

Firemen were on duty for twenty-four hour days and they lived on the second floor of the fire houses and when the alarm rang, requiring their services, the men would get dressed and slide down a brass pole. These men had a lot of time on their hands so to help alleviate the boredom or delinquency, Rober spent much of his spare time making medicine balls and promoting boxing matches. These sports didn't allow for mass participation so something needed to be done to allow for that.

Rober saw the need to incorporate the small vacant lot adjacent to the fire house to play a variation of baseball. He cut the base distances in half and the pitching distance down to thirty-five feet. He then created a smaller size medicine ball and using a wood lathe made a bat with a two inch diameter. The close proximity to the fire house allowed the men to get exercise and still be available should a fire occur. The game grew in popularity and quickly fire companies were playing the game.

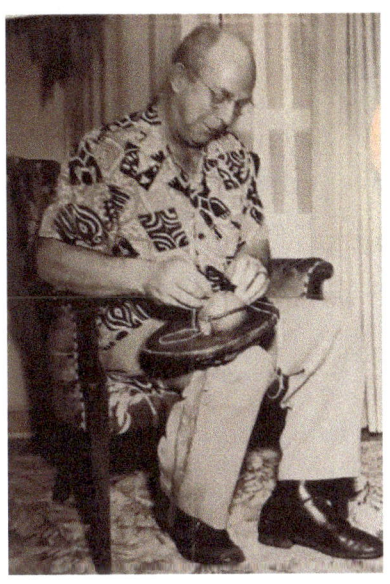

Lewis Roper sews a softball together

(photo on display in the USA Softball Hall Of Fame in Oklahoma City, Oklahoma.)

The next year, 1896, Rober was transferred to Fire Company No. 19 where he promptly organized a team called the "Kittens." The men of Fire Station No. 9 organized a team called the "Rats" and challenged the "Kittens" to a game. The "Kittens" won that game 5-0 and they were requested to play another game the following Saturday. The second game was won by the "Rats ", 4-2. About fifteen hundred people crowded around the field to watch each game.

By 1900, the popularity of the game caused a league to be formed. It was made up of: the "Kittens" of Engine House 19, the "Rats" of No. 9, the "Whales" of No. 4, plus the "Salisburys", "Pillsburys, and Central Avenues. A 12" circumference ball was used for these games. The games proved to be very competitive and usually played on Saturday afternoons. It was not unusual to have a crowd of 3,000 people at the playing field. Sometimes brothers would compete against each other being on different teams. The games were so intense that families divided on the merits of teams and some members would go through an entire season without speaking to one another.

By the summer of 1900 the league was called "Kitten League Ball" by Captain George Kehoe of Truck Company No. 1 in honor of Lieutenant Rober's original team. The league name was eventually shortened to "Kitten Ball". By 1913 numerous leagues were formed on city playgrounds and because of the limited space, equipment, and time, the game required athletic associations throughout the city.

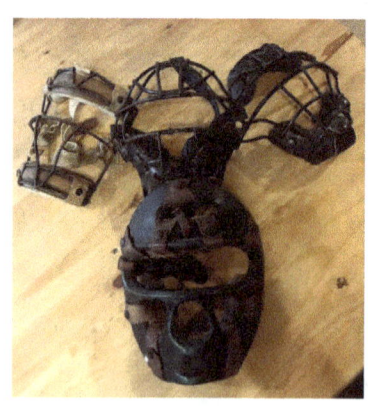

(circa 1890-1900's) used by either players or umpires

The St. Paul Pioneer Press on August 15, 1915 said the new game took over in Minneapolis' twin city, St. Paul. "Kitten Ball has at last come into its own in St. Paul. The popular game, a first cousin to the great American Sport and half brother to the indoor baseball game, has secured a foothold in this city. It has been played here for the past two or three years, but not until the Park Board officially recognized it at the start of the present season did it really display a healthy growth."

The newspaper went of to say, "Kitten Ball is faster than baseball. Games of nine innings duration have been frequently played in forty-five minutes. It is an ideal after-dinner sport which may be indulged in by any person, man or woman, without danger of injury or lameness." By the end of summer, nine leagues were finishing their schedules.

The year 1920 saw 64 men's teams in 11 divisions, and 25 girl's teams in four divisions entered under the Park Board. Rules of the game were changed very little from its inception years prior. The first rulebook, "Official Kitten Ball Guide", published in 1906 and in use today shows only minor changes. Compared to the year 1936 they were:

Baselines in 1906 – 45 feet, 1936 – 45 feet.

Pitching distance in 1906 – 35 feet, 1936 – 37 feet, 8 ½ inches.

Ball size in 1906 – 7 ounces, 13" in diameter, 1936 – 6 ounces, 12" in circumference.

Bat size in 1906 -34 inches in length, 2" circumference, 1936 – 34" in length, 2 ½"

In circumference.

Number of players in 1906 – 10, 1936 – 10.

Number of innings in 1906 – 9, 1936 – 7.

The Park authorities in 1922 felt the name "Kitten Ball" was not appropriate and changed it to "Diamond Ball". The "Tribune" quotes Minneapolis Director of Recreation, Karl Raymond: "Diamond Ball is not baseball. It finds its basis in baseball but it does not require the high degree of organization, nor the complete equipment that baseball requires. It is essentially a game of recreation. The longer baseline in baseball makes the game to difficult for girls, and also requires a larger area for play. Using the shorter distances, the game is much more adaptable for athletic recreation."

1908 Softball gets organized

Quickly the game spread to all areas of the country and the need to establish an organization became obvious. In 1908, an organization called the National Amateur Playground Ball Association of the United States was formed. Just by coincidence that organization preceded the Joint Rules Committee on Softball by fifteen years and the Amateur Softball Association of America by twenty-five years.

Of course it was formed in Chicago and it had national representation, a printed official handbook, plans for inter-city competition and the possibility of future growth. The rules printed in the 1908 handbook was published by the American Sports Publishing Company, and with few exceptions, are similar to the Official Rules of Softball for 1946. A few odd differences were:

1. The first batter to get on in an inning could run to either first or third base. All following runners in that innings had to run in the same direction.

2. A legal game consisted of five, seven or nine innings, at the option of the contesting teams.

3. The game could be played by points rather than runs if desired. A point was scored by each and every base reached by a runner.

4. The bases were thirty-five feet apart and the pitcher's box was thirty feet from the home plate. The ball could be anywhere from 12" to 14" in circumference. The bat was

restricted to a two inch diameter.

5. Only three unfairly delivered balls were required for a base on balls. A base runner could not leave his base until the ball crossed home plate.

The pioneers of the game witnessed the growth of the game, however, the growth and development of this national organization eventually ended and soon disappeared as an effective organization for promoting the game and securing a uniform set of rules.

This game with the shorter bases and larger ball was particularly adapted to playgrounds, and in the era following 1908 most municipalities recreation programs grew rapidly. With this grew the game, "Playground Ball." Spikes were not allowed, only the catcher and first baseman could wear gloves, and a runner could not score on a passed ball. The third strike was out even if the ball went ten feet over the catcher's head.

Ten players constituted a team and a new rule allowing bunting, made it necessary for two players to play close to home plate. These players were called the right and left short-stops. Outdoors the shortstop played in his normal position but the 10th player remained. He was called the shortfielder and could play anywhere in fair territory, but usually behind the infielders and in front of the outfielders.

When the game caught on, it was easily played outdoors, which basically ended the need for indoor softball. Playground leagues flourished all over the country but they were just a mish mash of teams just enjoying the game but intent on kicking the pants of rival teams. As newspapers encouraged the playing of the new game, recreation departments grew and became more interested in softball rather than the game of baseball.

Sponsors became the norm as businesses began seeing the usefulness of having their names on uniforms as a form of advertisement. Many colorful names sprung up on sweaters and sweatshirts and some teams even had the same sponsor as others. Softball was becoming a national sport.

What Happened to George Hancock?

On a strange side note, little is known about Mr. George W. Hancock's life after his invention of the game and the publication of his indoor-outdoor rules in 1889. It is unclear whether Hancock played a role in the future development of the game. It is also noteworthy that George W. Hancock is not enshrined in the National Softball Hall of Fame. He would be astonished to see his "game" is now played in over 100 countries around the world.

Photo of George Hancock

History of the Farragut Boat Club

The Farragut Boat Club was organized by a limited number of members in 1872. It began with a small boathouse at the foot of 12th Street and was renamed Roosevelt Road on May 25, 1919. Architect, Robert Rae Jr., a influential architect in Chicago in the late 1800s. The beautiful red brick, two story clubhouse was completed in the spring of 1886 and located at 413-415 Lake View Avenue (3016-3018 Lake Park Avenue today). It had a basement, balconies, and stone trimming.

Club officers were: Charles S. Downs, President; F. G. Whiting, Vice President; C.F. Bryant, Secretary; F.M. Staples, Treasurer; Charles De V. Hoard, Chairman Board of Admissions; George A. McClellan, Captain, Everett C. Brown, Commander; Ed S. Hunter, Lieutenant Commander; and George W. Hancock, Ensign (1890 Chicago Blue Book).

Photo of Farragut Boat Club

In the basement was a bowling alley, gymnasium, a pool room and lavatories. The first floor had parlors, a reception room, a billiard room, card room and a library.

The second floor had a stunning dance hall and brilliant theatre, with a full stock of scenery and props, and seating capacity of four hundred. The theatricals became known as some of the finest entertainment by amateur thespians. A series of entertainments was also presented each winter.

The boathouse was a one-story brick building located at the foot for 33rd Street. The club owned approximately twenty-five boats, including an eight-oared barge, four-oared shells, gigs, single and double shells and single and double training boats, along with pleasure boats of various kinds. Initiation fee to the Farragut Boat Club was $50 ($1,400 today) and yearly dues of $24 ($700 today).

Note: Robert Rae Jr. (c. 1853-1920) was born in Philadelphia and came to Chicago with his parents in 1860. His father was a prominent lawyer and he was educated in the public school system of Chicago and entered the office of architect Henry Lord Gay in 1872. Two years later he was appointed assistant chief engineer Of the Chicago & South Atlantic Railroad, a position he held for a number of years before starting his own architectural office in Chicago in about 1880. His practice focused on small scale commercial buildings and residences in historic styles.

This photo was taken around 1995 outside the "16-Inch Softball Hall of Fame" was this stone and brass "Farragut Boathouse Monument," which commemorates the birth of softball in Chicago in 1887. It was originally placed at 31st Street and Lake Park Avenue in Chicago

Photo of Monument

The location of the Farragut Boat Club is now just an empty lot. The affluent clubhouse was razed in 1952.

Chapter Two

The Depression, Softball and ASA

As the names, "kittenball", "Mushball", "Indoor ball" and others were no longer used, the name "softball" was now becoming the normal name for the new outdoor game. All of these names caused confusion and conflict and once again the need for an organization sprung up in none other than Springfield, Illinois in 1923.

At the National Recreation Congress, Joseph Lee, the leader of the playground movement to bring a standard to the game of softball. Recreation program directors, known as the Playground Baseball Committee, came from cities throughout the United States and they wanted uniformity to the game. After much deliberation, this committee finally agreed on and published an official set of rules and when returning urged their citizens to play the game under those rules. They were now called the Joint Rules Committee.

Walter L. Hakanson, a Young Man's Christian Association (YMCA) official and an active leader of the new game in Colorado, claimed that the name "Softball" originated at a meeting held in 1926 in Colorado. At an organization meeting in Chicago, in 1932, many names for the game were suggested and considered but it was finally decided to accept and adopt the name from Colorado and the sport has been nationally known as Softball from that day forward. There were many problems facing the committee as the game was being played in every town, village, and city in every state in the nation as well as some foreign countries. Various size softballs were being used as well a bat lengths, base lengths, and many variations of the original rules. Trying to establish a joint set of rules, standards and equipment was proving to be an enormous task.

Walter Hakanson ran state tournaments organized by the YMCA since 1926 and an accomplished athlete; three times all-city in football and four times all-city in basketball. He was also a very skilled official in football (445 games) and basketball (2,284 games) for twenty-five years. For forty-five years at the YMCA Hakanson was involved in many other sports such as, baseball, swimming, handball, volleyball and softball.

Ultimately it was softball that Hakanson achieved national recognition. At the 1926 Colorado Softball Committee meeting in Greeley, he "coined" the name "Softball." He stated in a newspaper article in 1946 that "Softball enjoyed its greatest season in history and the Amateur Softball Association (ASA) anticipated even greater things in 1947." He added, "Recreation and public officials were working diligently to keep up with the demand for diamonds. Two hundred and thirty-nine cities constructed seven-hundred and seventy-one diamonds yet they could not appease the cry, "Give us more places to play."

Harkanson held a joint position for the Colorado ASA, commissioner and secretary-treasurer, as he officially formed the

Colorado ASA in 1931. He served as president of the national ASA in 1948.

The Playground Baseball Committee of the National Recreation Association formed in 1923 by Joseph Lee, was enlarged later that year to include representatives of the Young Men's Christian Association (YMCA), the National Collegiate Athletic Association (NCAA), and the American Physical Education Association. It was called the Joint Rules Committee.

The Great Depression

Then came Black Friday, October 24, 1929. The beginning of the depression and how would it affect recreational and professional sports. The stock market officially crashed and stock plummeted and banks began to call in their loans from its clients to cover their losses. President Herbert Hoover stated that any lack of confidence in our economic future was "foolish". This became an obvious mistake as Americans faced what would be disastrous times. By 1930 unemployment would reach an estimated 4 million and that number would just increase for the next few years.

The golden years of baseball was peaking as Lou Gehrig and Babe Ruth were having home run battles. Americans went to see their "heroes" in droves to escape the gloom and doom of the depression. However, the sport was facing tough times as many new teams had built new stadiums or completed renovations on their facilities to support the growing number of fans.

With so many people looking for work, attendance dropped significantly by 40%. Salaries had to be cut to absorb the loses, by an average of 25% Even the great Babe Ruth took a dramatic pay decrease of 50% of his $80,000 salary. Minor league teams were forced into bankruptcy and even some Major League teams were looking at means to alleviate their financial losses.

While the politicians and bankers were trying to figure out how to survive, Americans turned to their radios or playgrounds as an escape mechanism. Recreational baseball and softball was being played everywhere as the horrors of empty wallets, due to no jobs available, and empty ice boxes, for lack of food became reality. America was in serious need of positive distractions, and the era provided many means of entertainment we enjoy today. The Major League All Star game, the National Football League Championship game, and the National Basketball League in 1937, formed from the Midwest Basketball Conference.

On December 14, 1930 Knute Rockne took his Notre Dame All Stars team to New York to play the New York Giants. It was billed as an event to raise money for the Committee on Unemployed and 55,000 fans showed up and more than $110,000 was raised. This was truly innovative as football was evolving into professionalism from collegiate play. Soon, the pros and college football would become vastly different from one another and the interest in each sport would gain enormous growth. By 1932 the National Football League adopted the forward pass from the quarterback from anywhere behind the line of scrimmage into the rules. This move obviously made professional football even more interesting.

By 1931 unemployment had risen to six million and by 1933 thousands of banks had shut their doors. The mood of suffering Americans began to worsen as Hoover believed the government should not intervene with the economy nor help create jobs. His decision led to the country deeper into the depression and by 1932 20% of the country became unemployed. Suicides soared as Americans saw no hope. The election year of 1933 proved that the people had enough of the Hoover administration and overwhelmingly elected Franklin D. Roosevelt to hopefully lead America out of the abyss.

The year 1933 proved to be the worst year for professional baseball. Salaries were cut so badly, that teams were looking for players willing to accept a minimal wage. Many players saw their pay cut by 25% but they were still lucky to have a job. Players flocked to Florida during the spring of 1934 in hopes of getting signed, believing even a small salary was better than none at all. The average wage for an American fell 50% during this time and a player making just $3,000 was still making twice as much as the typical industrial worker. Hoping the Roosevelt administration would help solve its problems proved more dismal, as the first 100 days the depression was just getting worse.

The Amateur Softball Association Forms

Efforts to create a true softball association was a struggle. Two men from Chicago came up with an ingenious idea. With the World's Fair coming to Chicago in the summer of 1933, Leo Fischer and Maurice (Mike) J. Pauley decided to host a massive softball tournament. Believing this would prove to be sensational to have teams from all over the country meet and compete and have them agree to split into separate statewide organizations and agree to a national governing body. Indoor softball was now being played in mass outdoors.

Photo of Leo Fischer and M. J Pauley

Photo of softball being played indoors

An invitation from the organizers of the Chicago World's Fair for Fischer, assistant sports editor for the "Chicago American", and Pauley, a sporting goods salesman to organize and host a softball tournament. This would be held on September 2 – 9 using a diamond built under one of the huge sky-ride towers. Fischer wrote in his book, "Winning Softball", "M.J. Pauley and I were asked to conduct it because of our success with a local tournament in Chicago in which more than 1,000 teams participated."

Imagine the difficult task before these two men? They had 10 days and $500 from the organizers along with one of the worst years of the Great Depression, to organize this event. How do you get the information out to teams in many states that all play under different rules, sizes of softballs, and different base and pitching distances? It seemed to be a monumental disaster in the making.

Sitting down they quickly wrote an arbitrary set of rules to present to the teams. A 14 inch ball would be used along with 60 foot bases. Equipment would be standardized and games would be seven innings long except for the semi-finals and championship games.

Chicago World's Fair A Century of Progress Poster

World's Fair organizers were extremely skeptical that Fischer and Pauley could pull this off. Pauley wrote in his book, "Worth Book of Softball" that the efforts of Fischer was what made their idea grew into something even they never thought would happen. "He wrote stories tirelessly and besieged wire services with articles, which they took only as a favor to him and not because they thought that softball deserved the time and money it required to send the stories out."

Pauley continued, "We climbed into the car and every state we heard of where any kind of softball tournament was being conducted, the winning team was invited to this first national softball championship event. The meet attracted a grand total of fifty-five team) to play in a single elimination tournament. They came from Colorado, Louisiana, Georgia, Connecticut, Kentucky, Illinois, Indiana and nine other states. We had a cross-section of the nation represented."

The teams were told there would be no free room and board nor travel money as the entire $500 was used up. There was just enough money left to purchase trophies. Teams began arriving by car, train, and some by bicycles and they slept in tents and ate bologna sandwiches. "It is the largest and most comprehensive tournament ever staged in the sport which has swept the country like wildfire," wrote the "Chicago American".

"Fifty title winners from Colorado to New Jersey and from Minnesota to Florida have sent their winners. The diamond is located on Northerly Island, near the east town of the Sky Ride and bleacher space is available for thousands of spectators," the newspaper added.

There would be three divisions of play; Men's fast pitch, slow pitch and women's softball as the organizers didn't want to leave the female players out. Fischer said, "We didn't think the girls game would go well, but we didn't want to slight them. They could have the chance, if they wanted it. It developed that they wanted it, and the play for the ladies' championship game of 1933 really featured our program."

Unemployment was well over 20% when the Chicago World's Fair began and plenty of Americans had a lot of free time on their hands. The World's Fair offered free admission and over 350,000 people attended the event. What was truly stunning was 70,000 fans attended the first round of the single-elimination softball national tournament. Thousands more continued to attend the games and when it ended there was no doubt that the game of softball had grabbed the nation and it would have a great future.

The championship games were played at Chicago's Stadium on September 15. Chicago's Great Northern Laundry won the women's division 18-3, and the Friedman Boosters prevailed over Briggs Beauty Ware from Detroit, 5-1 in the men's slow pitch division as Harry (Coon) Rosen tossed a one-hitter. It was the first loss of the season for Briggs after 41 consecutive wins. There is no known record of who won the men's fast pitch division.

Photos of the Chicago Symphony Orchestra softball players

A strange side story: A special softball game was played between the Chicago Symphony Orchestra and the Detroit Symphony Orchestra on Monday, July 23, 1934 which was still part of the Chicago World's Fair as it went on for a full year. The Chicago team winning 18-17, when cellist player, Don Seidenburg, hit a tie breaking home run in the seventh inning to win the game. He is pictured below.

Dan Seidenberg, first cellist, whose home run blast to deep center field at Grant Park shattered a deadlocked softball game between the Chicago

Photo of Don Seidenburg

The Chicago Symphony Orchestra played twice daily at the Swift bandshell during the World's Fair while the Detroit Symphony Orchestra was filling a long engagement at Ford Gardens, also at the World's Fair. It is safe to assume a challenge was probably issued between them to play a game of softball. That game was played at Grant Park and many spectators attended.

The huge success of this first national tournament convinced Fischer and Pauley that America needed a national softball organization. They set up an office in the Morrison Hotel in Chicago with Fischer being the president without a salary and Pauley serving as executive secretary. Although the new organization had no funding, Pauley was given a full-time salary of $2,600. Thus began the organization which would become the "Amateur Softball Association."

Fischer and Pauley's first order of business was to raise money to help support their new organization. The Athletic Institute and "Chicago American" agreed to help with the financing and this enabled the two men to form associations and appoint commissioners nationwide. The Athletic Institute contributed $5,200 each year through 1938 and the "Chicago American" paid the utility bills, including lights and a telephone.

1933 was a banner year for softball's new governing body. Fischer wrote in his book, "Winning Softball" that "The tournament was successful enough, but it was also a turning point in the game of softball. It brought home the need for uniformity in rules."

It was apparent that the organization needed to hold its first rules meeting at Chicago's Hotel Sherman. This meeting led to the formation of the International Joint Rules Committee on

Softball (IJRCS). It is widely accepted that this meeting helped to alleviate the confusion of all the different rules being used in other states. The next meeting was scheduled in early 1934 and it was decided the new organization needed to be non-profit and Clarence Brewer of Detroit, Michigan was elected as chairman, by the 200 representatives in attendance.

It was decided to endorse another national tournament in 1934 as interest was still at an apex. Fischer and Pauley contacted the "Chicago American" publisher, William Randolf Hearst to help defray the cost of hotel rooms and provide some entertainment for the 1,001 players who would be playing and he obliged with a donation of $7,000..Teams were still required to fund their own travel expenses. Hearst also agreed to promote the event and contributed $50,000 through 1938. The Chicago Parks District actually set up the diamonds needed at no cost.

A total of thirty-two teams representing twenty-five states played in this tournament and all games were played during the daytime. The Ke-Nash-A Motormakers of Kenosha, Wisconsin defeated the Crimson Coaches team from Toledo, Ohio, 2-0 in the men's championship game. The Hart Motor Girls of Chicago beat Gem City from Dayton, Ohio, 5-1 in the women's championship game. The Ke-Nash-A Motormakers team was presented the William Randolf Hearst trophy. It was thirty-seven inches tall, with solid gold and ebony figurines on the handles. It was valued at $1,000 and probably is priceless today.

Like the previous year admission was free and over 200,000 fans attended the three day event. Major League Baseball commissioner, Judge Kenesaw Mountain Landis and his wife were also in attendance. So enthralled with the game, Mrs. Landis decided to pass on a "dinner date" by her husband so she could stay and watch the competition. Judge Landis even sat on the bench of the Ke-Nash-A motormakers bench during the championship game. He then told a reporter for the "Chicago American" that he didn't believe the game of softball would hurt baseball. "Any game that can interest fans is bound to help the enthusiasm for any sport." He stated.

Judge Landis went so far as to ask Rip Collins, a member of the St. Louis Gas House Gang (a nickname for the Cardinals) to try and hit a softball pitched to him.

"Ripper do you think you can hit that big ball?" Landis asked.

"Pardon the expression, Judge, but hell, I can't even see the ball." Collins responded.

Twenty-two ASA commissioners attended the games and saw an opportunity to make recommendations on how to improve the game. One of these was how to get more offense into the game so they came to an agreement to move the pitching distance from 37 feet 8 and ½ inches to 40 feet. The "Playground Association Softball Guide" proclaimed: "The promotional activities of the Amateur Softball Association of America played an important part in stimulating the interest that had been developing for many years."

The Joint Rules Committee met in Washington, D.C., in October of 1934 during the Recreation Congress. It was decided to invite other softball organizations, so the National Softball Association (NSA), Amateur Softball Association of America (ASA), Catholic Youth Organization and the Young Men's Hebrew Association were invited to attend. It was recommended that the Joint Rules Committee of Softball be reorganized and a permanent incorporated organization be established. This organization would add prestige, greater representation and ensure softball to grow.

One important item that needed to be addressed was one set of rules be adopted and published. Principal sports equipment manufacturers were given support that any rules published for this game would be in accord with the official rules published by the Joint Rules Committee. The Amateur Softball Association of America was officially recognized as the organization that could accomplish this.

The game of softball which is generally played recreationally, has now become one of the favorite sports to play. Like baseball, it was accepted nationally and played by athletic clubs all over America.

Several photos of various types of equipment used by players.

The second national tournament in 1934 became a major turning point for ASA. Fischer wrote, "The tournament also served to put firmly on the map the Amateur Softball Association of America, which in one year has stepped forward to be recognized as the governing body of the sport, with affiliated bodies in 35 states, with others certain to line up before the next year." It was obvious the 1933 tournament was ground breaking and the 1934 tournament established the ASA as an organization.

The year 1936 was a memorable one for many reasons. The national tournament was once again held in Chicago with the Kodak Park team from Rochester, New York winning it all. Harold "Shifty" Gears pitched through the rain to lead his team and became the first Eastern team to win the title.. Note: Harold Gears would become the very first inductee into the ASA National Softball Hall of Fame in 1957.

Although the new organization would end up in the red by $7,547.57 when the tournament finished, ASA still made progress and established in forty-one states and 10 metro associations. ASA estimated that 92,454 teams played 1,850,000 softball games in America before over 185 million people. Also the 12 inch, smooth seam ball was now their official ball. The forty-five foot diamond was replaced with the sixty foot diamond. As suggested in 1934, the pitching distance was moved to 40 feet.

During the tournament, the ASA elected sectional vice-presidents. Named were: Walter Hakanson, Denver, Colorado (Western),

Harold B. Dow, Westport, Connecticut (Eastern), Early Maxwell, Memphis, Tennessee (Southern) and Seth Whitmore, Lansing, Michigan (Central). The "Chicago American" was contacted to help bail ASA out of the red for the tournament and the newspaper agreed under the condition that the sum be deducted from the 1937 tournament prior to any profit being realized.

1934 also saw another type of pitch other than the widely accepted "figure eight". Crafty pitchers such as; Harold "shifty" Gears, Harry Kraft, George Manrose, Carl "two-gun Hunt, Casey Drop and Cam Ecclestone were some of the best at using the figure eight. During the World Championship games, Paul Watson of Arizona introduced the "windmill" pitch. This pitch caused confusion with batters as they didn't know when he would deliver the pitch. Only Watson knew just how many rotations he would use before actually pitching. Also, Watson at times would start behind the pitching plate and step forward placing a foot on the pitching plate before starting the windup. *It wasn't long before a rule was put in place allowing for only one windmill rotation.

Every pitcher realizes he can't just rely on the fast pitch to win games. A repertoire of an assortment of pitches is necessary, such as the rise ball, curve, drop and change up. It doesn't matter if the pitcher uses a wind up, figure eight, or straight forward delivery, a pitcher realizes he needs so-called "stuff" to beat the opponent.

An article in "Softball" newsletter stated, "The umpires will have plenty to do this year in calling illegal pitching. This year the new rule will be any illegal pitch may be called by the umpire unless the batsman hits the ball into fair territory. An illegally pitched ball struck at and missed, or fouled, and an illegally pitched ball struck at and missed shall be called a ball.".

Whitmore added, "In pitching the windup may consist of not more than one upward in front and over, or one downward and backward swing of the pitching arm. The ball shall be delivered on the first forward swing of the pitching arm. It is believed that the 1936 rule changes will put more action in the game and create an even greater following."

As the Depression draws to an end, ASA grows

After 1935 the need for diversion in sports coupled with increased governmental support for recreational activities improved opportunities for sports in America. The depression impacted the preferred sports of the wealthy. Country club membership dropped, many clubs closed, golf tournaments were cancelled and prizes were drastically cut. The United States Golf Association (USGA) included 1,134 affiliated clubs in 1930, but by 1936 there were only 763.

Interest in bowling, softball, and basketball for men and bowling, softball and tennis grew tremendously during this time. It required less skill and space for these sports. Bowling and softball could also be played at night as lighted parks were being built quickly. In the crowded inner cities, pool halls and bowling remained important hangouts. Bowling, for instance, rebounded in the late 30's as the number of registered teams tripled. Chicago alone had over nine hundred leagues and over 4,000 bowling alleys with receipts of nearly $49 million. By 1939 the purse for the American Bowling Congress (ABC) reached $170,000.

During the depression years, FDR's "New Deal" built numerous community recreational facilities financed with $750 million. The "Works Progress Administration (WPA) promoted sports, such as softball, by building 770 swimming pools and 5,898 athletic fields. The "Civilian Conservation Corps" (CCC) built ski runs, camp grounds and boating facilities. The number of cities sponsoring public recreation programs between 1934 and 1936 doubled to 2,190. Expenditures on recreation programs in the United States rose from $27 to $42 million during those years and reached $57 million by 1940.

Professional and Commercial sports suffered the most during the Great Depression, but managed to rebound by the mid-30's. Major League's baseball teams from New York actually banned radio from broadcasting games from 1934-1939. Night baseball was introduced following the model of the Kansas City Monarchs of the Negro National League (NNL). In 1935 the Cincinnati Redlegs became the first major league team to play night games. No other teams followed their lead until 1938. Another promotional aspect by major league baseball was the founding of the Baseball Hall of Fame in 1936, located in Cooperstown, New York.

Horse racing also suffered during the early 30's which saw revenue drop by almost 50% in 1933. The Belmont Stakes, in New York City, dropped from $66,040 in 1930 to $35,480 in 1935. Earnings did not return to 1930 levels until 1937 but by 1939 they were up to $15.9 million. College football was severely hurt as by the fall of 1932 attendance dropped by 20% and many institutions considered dropping the sport. By 1935 the sport recovered and reached its pre-Depression level. Warm climate cites chose to promote tourism by offering "bowl games". Miami inaugurated the Orange Bowl in 1933, New Orleans followed in 1935 with the Sugar Bowl, El Paso with the Sun Bowl in 1936 and Dallas with the Cotton Bowl in 1937.

The National Football League began to see an upsurge in interest after the 1934 college football all-star game. In 1936 the NFL initiated a draft of college seniors to equalize competition. This helped collegiate players secure off-season employment. Basketball was taking a strong foothold and sportswriter Ned Irish, was encouraged to promote intersectional college doubleheaders in 1934. The first national tournament, the National Invitational Tournament (NIT) started in 1938 in New York City. The National Collegiate Athletic Association (NCAA) began theirs in 1939. That year also saw the Harlem Globetrotters win the first Chicago World Professional tournament.

Boxing was one of few sports which benefitted from the hard times of the depression. Tough inner-city Jewish, Italian, Irish and African-American youths attempted to escape poverty through prize fighting. There were about 8,000 professional boxer during the 30's and competition was fierce. Arguably Joe Louis, from Detroit, was a huge factor in encouraging suffering Americans. People would gather around radios in their living rooms and on porches to hear the broadcast of his fights. Louis won the World Championship in 1938 by knocking out James Braddock.

However, it was the much anticipated re-match with Max Schmeling that truly brought the nation together. Schmeling had beaten Louis in 1936 and the re-match drew 70,000 fans to Yankee Stadium in New York City and countless millions to their radios to hear the fight. The match had heavy political ramifications because it symbolized the conflict between German Nazism and American democracy. Louis represented the hopes of all Americans regardless of race, and his first-round knockout of Schmeling was widely regarded as a vindication of the American way of life.

All of these important sports and recreational activities helped Americans to put the Great Depression behind them. Softball continued to grow as a recreational sport and so did ASA. A thirty-two page publication, "Softballs and Strikes" is introduced in 1937 that highlights the national championship. The publication is Discontinued in 1942 but revitalized in 1947 with the present day name of "Balls and Strikes."

The 1937 ASA men's championship was highlighted by the shortest men's fast pitch softball game in only twenty-seven minutes. Norbert "Cyclone" Warken, pitching for Curlee Clothing Company of Covington, Kentucky struck out fourteen batters and allowed only one hit while defeating Denver, Colorado. Curlee finished fifth in the tournament but Warken struck out sixty-six batters in just four games and pitched two no-hitter, including the tournament's only perfect game, all in the same day! National championships in Chicago are carried play-by-play over the radio, a first for the game of softball.

These championship tournaments proved to be quite popular with the players and fans, but they still weren't making a profit. The ASA once again had to acquire financial assistance from the "Chicago American", which paid off the $1,062,87 deficit. This newspaper actually spent close to $30,000 to help stage the first six tournaments in Chigao (1933-1938).

The year 1938 was described as the greatest season in the history of softball according to the inaugural edition of the "Softball" magazine published in January of 1939. Over 100 milllion fans attended games andThe World Championship games in Chicago drew teams from all over the country and crowned the Polher's team of Cincinnati and Krieg's women's team from Alameta, California as champions. The Krieg's team became the first team from outside the mid-west to win the championship since it began in 1933.

Hundreds of new facilities were built and thousands of teams organized to play the great game. Although impossible to obtain actual figures on the growth of softball, it should be noted that not a single state reported a decline in interest. Major growth was in the south. The International Harvester team from Little Rock, Arkansas as well as women's teams from southern Texas proved how the interest in the south has taken off.

Over a dozen new rules were adopted in late 1938, and the most important were; catchers were mandated to wear masks and the women also had to wear chest protectors. Also adopted were:

Rule 8, Section C – Add – "the pitcher must release the ball simultaneously with the forward step." Penalty is an illegal pitch.

Rule 9, Add a new Section 9 – "It is an illegal pitch if a pitcher continues the windup after taking the step towards the batter."

Rule 16, Add to the first paragraph, "Any foul tip caught is a strike and the ball remains in play whether it is the 1st, 2nd, or 3rd strike."

Rule 20, Section 8 – Add – "a bunted fly ball" shall not be considered an infield fly.'

Rule 23, Add a new section – "The ball remains in play when a runner leaves a play too soon."

Rule 29, - Add – "A baserunner, having acquired the right to run to first base is to be called out if he runs to any other than first base."

Rule 31, Section 6 – Is removed of Rule 31 and put under a new heading, "Protests."

A move to eliminate the short fielder and establish nine men as official was defeated by a vote of 8 to 4. Representatives from Michigan, Minnesota, Florida, and California voted for nine players.

Michigan was a leader in breaking the "color barrier" when the ASA decided to accept the invitation of the Michigan Softball Association to host the "World's Colored Softball Championships". It was held in Memphis, Tennessee in 1937 but no tournament was held in 1938. The tournament will be awarded to the city making the best bid, and it is believed this will be either Flint or Pontiac. The Big Six team of Pontiac currently holds the title.

In 1938, the ASA established its Board of Governors (later known as the executive Board or Board of Directors) and assigned President Fischer chairman of that board. This is also the first year that ASA reported a profit: Income was reported as $9,573.94 and expenses were $9,339.11 showing cash on hand as $234.83. Also the association became a member of the American Olympic Association, and in the opinion of the officers of ASA, it will not be long before softball will be included in the Olympic games.

NOTE: In 1937, a retired Babe Ruth accepted the challenge to face a 25 year old softball pitcher named John Cannon Ball Baker, at a charity event. The great Babe swung and missed on 15 consecutive pitches. He would become the first of many major league baseball players to have difficulty hitting a fast pitch softball over the years.

Chapter Three

Michigan Amateur Softball Association Begins

The Michigan Amateur Softball Association (MASA) was founded in the spring of 1934 after the organization of the Amateur Softball Association in Chicago the previous fall. Prior efforts to organize the softball interests of the state into a unified body failed because various cities could not agree on a name of the rules which the game was to be played.

Softball was being played in Michigan in 1933 under various names ranging from "kitten ball" to "diamond ball" and "playground ball". There was so many different sets of rules and inter-city play was almost impossible. When the Joint Rules Committee was established and ASA founded, it became apparent to organize the different cities. Some disliked giving up their pet names for the game, but finally all agreed on the title of Softball, and newspapers, especially sports editors, were glad to see this name change after struggling to get other names in headings.

Michigan was a pioneer in the organization in the establishment of districts and regions and today is still one of few states that conducts softball tournament competition in more than four classes. There are men and women fast and slow pitch, industrial, coed, modified classes and youth tournaments in eight different classes.

On Thursday, May 24, 1934 the State Journal of Lansing reported that the softball season was starting the following week. Games were to played at Ranney Park and a new field located on the west side. "Several important games are scheduled for the first week on both sides of the city. What is supposed to be the biggest attraction will be the renewal of rivalry between the Oldsmakers and The State Journal at the west side field on Thursday night. The J.C. Penney team, defending champions of the higher league and Fisher Body, winners of the Class A title last year, will play at the same field Wednesday night."

The newspaper added, "On Tuesday night at Ranney Park, The State Journal will play Kellog's, league leaders of Battle Creek. However, the feature game on this night will be a girls game between Van's Hardware 10 and the Kellog Lassies, which will start at 7:30 preceding the Journal-Kellog contest."

Ten Years of Progress In Lansing

The buildings pictured above represent 10 years of development at the softball parks operated by the city recreation department of Lansing, Michigan. The upper left shows the first permanent scorer's box that was erected at Ranney park. It was constructed about eight years ago and succeeded an ordinary park bench. It is still used today, however, at one of the less important diamonds. The building at the upper right was set-up on the lighted West Side diamond, but it has grown obsolete and will likely be replaced before another season is here. Lower left is the present building at Ranney park where finals of the state championships are played. The most modern of all the buildings is shown at the lower right. Located at the new Elm Street lighted park, it is a fully equipped octagon structure. The buildings used at the lighted parks have sound systems, electric score boards, a press box, and other facilities. They are all located directly behind the home plates.

Photo of first Softball building

It should be noted that the Ranney Park field was the where the first softball building in America according to the State Journal. It was erected by the city of Lansing recreation department. This is most likely the original building which is located behind the backstop at Ranney field and still in use today.

Seth Whitmore, an editorial writer for the Lansing Journal was the first state commissioner and the organizer of MASA and also created the newsletter, "Softball". There were no District meets and all teams were invited to come to Lansing for the state finals. Forty-nine teams from sixteen town responded. Other leaders involved in the formation of MASA were: Lee Bancroft, Henry Croll, Mrs. H. R. Harvey, Herbert Kipke, Walter Smith, Arch Flannery, L. P. Moser, Lyle Hunt, and David (Bud) Brown.

Whitmore started playing softball when it was introduced in St. Petersburg, Florida, as "diamond ball" and followed the game for years. Not only did he organize the Michigan Softball association, but also became one of the vice presidents of ASA shortly thereafter. He actively played in the Lansing Triple A league for years. Under his leadership softball had districts formed with commissioners and state championship tournaments flourished as teams from all over the state came to Lansing too play. So popular was the game, that bleachers needed to be built to accommodate the thousands of spectators who would flock to watch their favorite teams and players.

Big Six team from Michigan

The official car of the Michigan Softball Association of Michigan was a 1934 Oldsmobile which was presented to Seth Whitmore. Oldsmobile, built in Lansing, would be the official car for many decades.

The first softball state tournaments were held in Lansing in the late summer of 1934. Gulf Refiners of Flint won the men's championship and Chrysler of Detroit won the first women's championship.

1935

In early April of 1935, Whitmore announced completion plans for the upcoming season. He stated that he expected a 50% increase in the number of teams in the state over the first year, this was based on the number of queries which had been received at his office. The second annual state tournament will again be held on Labor Day weekend with the finals set for September 2nd. All district tournaments must be completed by August 24 which will allow 32 teams from the men's and women's divisions to play. The winners in each division will represent Michigan at the National Tournament to be played in Chicago.

All teams must be members of the association and local amateur associations and an entry charge of $5 per team for the state tournament. All men's games will be played on a sixty foot diamond with forty foot pitching distance and all women's games will be played on a forty-five foot diamond as called for by the national association rules.

An amazing feat was already being reported early in the season by the "State Journal of Lansing" on June 17. Archie Tarpoff of the Lansing Oldsmobile team on top of the Triple A League has tossed six consecutive shutouts which is a record. A total of fifty consecutive innings, 18 of which where he only allowed three hits, and averaged just over 17 strikeouts per game. His team was favored again in 1935 to win it all.

Seth Whitmore told the United Press that all eighteen districts would begin district softball tournaments by August 17. With more than 300 teams already registered in the state, "200 teams are expected to qualify" with the deadline for filing to play would be August 16. He added, "The runner-up in the men's state tournament in addition to the Michigan championship game for the women would make the trip to Chicago if they so choose. The winners from the eighteen districts along with the runner-ups from the fourteen largest districts will compete in the state tournament but a limit of twenty women's teams has been set." Dozens of teams that waited until after the deadline to enter were rejected.

After the district tournaments finished on August 24, a total of 52 teams qualified for the state tournament, 32 men's teams and 20 women's teams. The 20 women's teams is a record. Games will be played at Ranney park and West side field and Marshall field and Bancroft park will be used as they have 24,000 watts of lights for nighttime play. Each champion will be presented the Oldsmobile trophy for permanent possession.

Herbert Kipke, left, chief official for the city recreational department of Lansing, and Marjara Miller, one of the capitol city's fairest hurlers, are shown above with the trophies that will be awarded to Michigan's 1936 softball champions at the third annual state tournament which opens at Lansing Friday, and closes with the title battles on the night of Labor Day. The two center trophies are awarded by Oldsmobile for the Class A championship, while those at the ends in the picture are the VanDervoort Class B awards. All will be given for permanent possession.

Photo of Oldsmobile trophies

The 1934 champions in the women's division, Chrysler of Detroit will not be included as Wayne County has formed their own association. It appears the strongest teams in the women's division will be the Shamrocks from Port Huron, Fisher Body and Reed's Shoes from Flint, the Moose team from Bay City and Van's of Lansing. Unlike the men's tournament, the women's division is comprised by any feminine team that wanted to play as it is an invitational tournament.

The Gulf Refineries of Flint will return to defend their 1934 title as they won their district title. They will be the favored team because of Ted Soroka, the sensational fast ball pitcher. He pitched the Flint team with three shutouts in five games last year. This year he tossed five no hitters! It won't be easy for the Gulf Refineries teams though, as the Lansing Oldsmobile team with outstanding thrower, Archie Tarpoff, will also return along with the Cut Rate Cigars team from Ann Arbor and fireballer, Estil Tessmer. Oldsmobile defeated the Gulf team twice in inter-city competition this year, but everyone knows that means little when the state tournament begins.

Whitmore said he expects enormous crowds for the event as softball has really caught on in the state. The Lansing park department has nearly 10,000 bleacher seats at Ranney Park and the West Side field. When the semi-final and championship games are set, they will be played at Ranney Park and all bleachers will be moved there in anticipation of huge crowds.

ASA Announces World Tournament Plans

The World Tournament of the Amateur Softball Association will once again be held in Chicago on September 7, 8, and 9. Winners of state tournaments and metropolitan districts throughout the country will battle for the right to be called champions. There is no entry fee, but dues from the state organizations must be paid before their teams will be allowed to compete.

The Hotel LaSalle will be the official headquarters for the teams. Hotel rooms will be provided for players and managers for all teams each night and for those who play on Monday, September 9, their rooms will be available for that night also. Accommodations for each state commissioner will be provided at the Belmont hotel on Lake Shore Drive.

The first games will begin on Saturday, September 7 at 11 a.m. and mayor Edward F. Kelly will be at the event to greet the teams. Losers in the first round will play a consolation game and the semi-finals and championships will take place on Monday, September 9. All games will be played in the daylight. The 12 inch ball will be used and pitching distance shall be 37 feet, 8 and one-half inches. All rules established by the Joint Rules Committee will be in effect. The tournament will be held under the auspices of the "Chicago American". The women and men will be playing at the same time and the same provisions will be made for the women's teams.

The winner will be presented the William Randolf Hearst national championship trophy to be kept for one year and individual trophies will be given to each player. A replica of the Hearst trophy will be given to each champion for their permanent possession.

Men's & Women's Brackets Set for state tournament

The first annual tournament in 1934 had no teams further north than Muskegon. Most of the contestants came from Saginaw, Flint, and central Michigan. Players will register at the fields they will be playing. The official headquarters will be at the city recreation department office at city hall and offices will be available with telephone communication at each playing location. New this year will be the use of three umpires each game rather than two from the previous year. It is expected that total attendance could top 30,000.

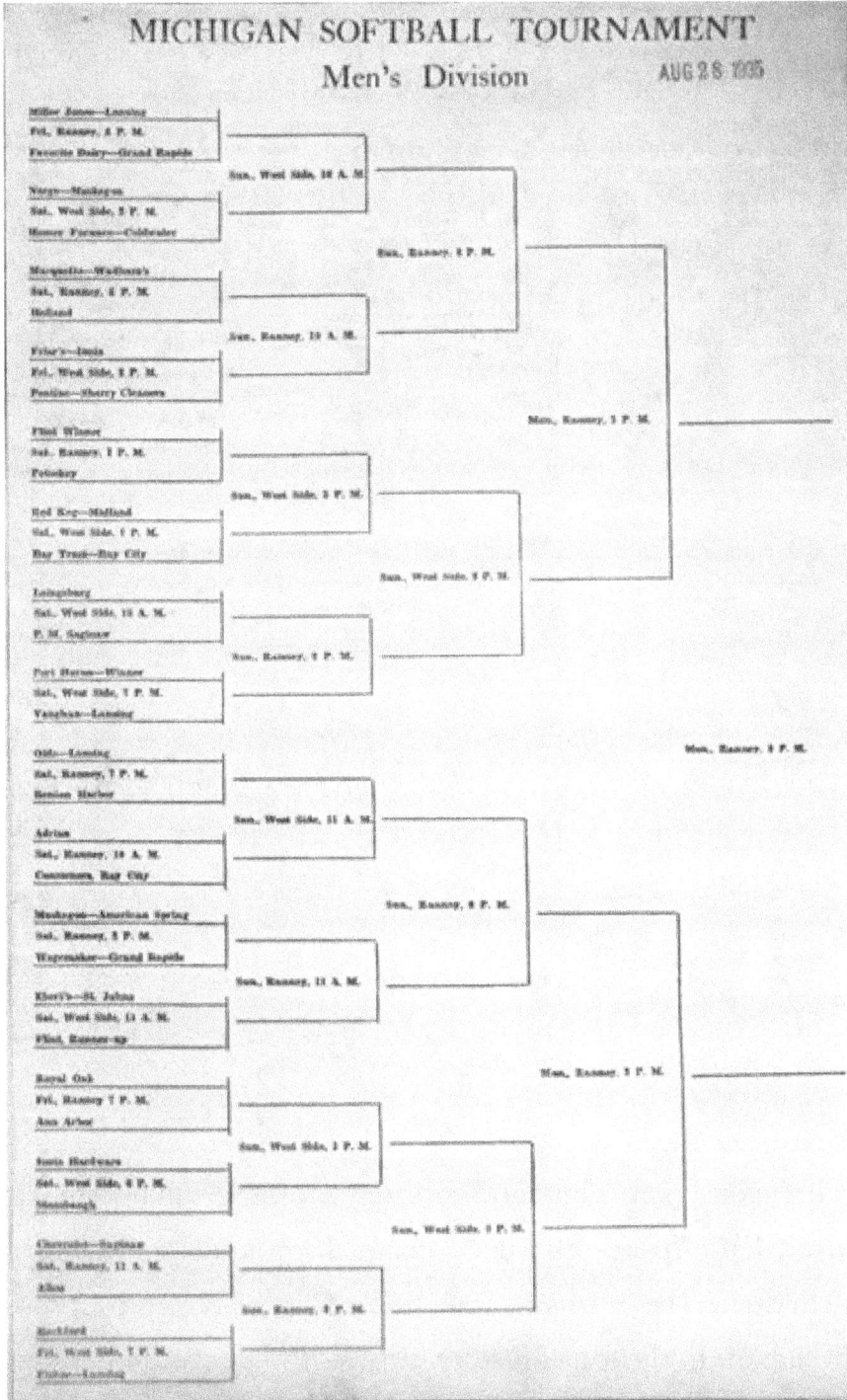

Photo of men's bracket

Photo of women's bracket

Admission Friday night and Saturday morning will be free, after that a twenty-five cents will be charged for adults and ten cents for children. The tournament has been billed as the greatest sports tournament in the state's history.

1935 State Tournament

Rain on Friday night didn't stop play as eight men's teams were eliminated and one team forfeited. The outstanding performance of the night was by Estil Tessmer, former Michigan football star, who tossed a two hit shutout for Cut Rate Cigars over the Royal Oak Fish and Poultry Ten. In the women's division, three Lansing teams and one from Grand Rapids walked away winners. Isabel Peters of Daniels Jewelry turned in a two-hitter in a 18-1 romp over Edwards Brothers from Ann Arbor.

The second round of play saw both 1934 champions eliminated. The Bay Trust team from Bay City, pounded Ted Sorocka for 9 hits and defeated Gulf Refiners, 5-0. Charles Martindale of the Bay Trust team tossed a three hitter to get the victory. Flint's Fisher Body team, the other finalist from 1934 lost to Chevrolet Standards of Saginaw, 5-3. Six of the eight games played were shutouts as pitching dominated play. Outstanding hurlers, Archie Tarpoff of the Lansing Oldsmobile team beat Consumer Power of Bay City, 6-0, and Estil Tessmer of Cut Rate Cigar shutout Ionia Hardware, 5-0. The toughest loss of the tournament occurred when the Bay City Trust team was eliminated in nine innings by Vaughan of Lansing 1-0. Martindale had a no-hitter going into the ninth, but a walk followed by the only hit drove in the winning run.

Winners of the second round for the women were Legion, Lansing over Reed's Flint 8-6 in nine innings, Oldsmobile, Lansing

6 edged Shamrocks of Port Hurton, 6-5, City Transport, Lansing, trounced Fisher Body, Flint, 16-4, and Van's from Lansing beat Moose of Bay City 8-4. This resulted in an all Lansing semi-final pairing for the Finals.

More than 4,000 fans showed up at Ranney Park to watch the men's semi-finals and finals on Sunday, September 1st. Oldsmobile of Lansing edged Chevrolet Standard of Saginaw 1-0 in a semi-final game. Vaughan of Lansing took advantage of poor fielding by Norge of Muskegon to win 3-2 in the other semi-final. That set up an all Lansing final between Vaughan and Oldsmobile.

The women's semi-finals saw the Transport team of Lansing defeating City champs, Van's 9-7 and Oldsmobile shutout the American Legion team of Lansing 6-0 behind a two-hit performance by Mary Ellen McKeon. The championship game later that night had the Transport team win a thriller against Oldsmobile 7-6. Pauline Richardson was outstanding for the Transport team pitching three games in 24 hours against very strong competition and winning all three games.

SEP 3 1935

Pitching three games within 24 hours, comely Pauline Richardson, above, led the City Transport team of Lansing to the girls' state softball championship. She hurled four victories in as many games, turning back the Salzburgh Merchants of Bay City, Flint Fisher Body, the champions of that city; VanDervoort Hardware, champions of Lansing, and Oldsmobile Six, runners-up for the state title. The City Transport team hit hard and fielded well behind Miss Richardson's skillful pitching. The team will represent Michigan in the world's championship tournament at Chicago this week-end. Miss Richardson is employed by the City Transport corporation.

Photos of Pauline Richardson

The men's championship game was historic as Archie Tarpoff of the Oldsmobile Six team tossed a no-hitter against Vaughan winning 1-0, as only two runners reached first base. It was Tarpoff's fourth shutout in five games proving how dominate he was. Jimmy Dyer, who threw for Vaughans also had an outstanding tournament as he only gave up three runs in five games. What is truly amazing about what Tarpoff did, is this is was his first year pitching softball after failing to make good at baseball.

The two state champions will now travel to Chicago to compete in the World Championship tournament for ASA. More than 50 people are expected to travel to Chicago to watch their favorite teams play.

1936

The third annual meeting and banquet scheduled for February 22 in 1936 had to be postponed due to heavy snow. The state association grew from 1,000 members in 1934 to 5,000 by the end of 1935. At the March 7 meeting, Commissioner Seth Whitmore reappointed ten district commissioners; John Erickson, Muskegon, Casimer Jablonski, Bay City, Rudolph Schmeling, Saginaw, Louis Hollway, Ann Arbor, F. C. Siddall, Reading, A. W. Thompson, Grand Rapids, Foster Kenny, Ionia, Harold C. Bradfield, Niles, George Zorn, Ishpeming, Herbert Kipke, Lansing and one new one, Archie Flannery in Battle Creek. The rest of the district commissioners will be named later in the week it was reported.

The Michigan Softball Association would meet in Lansing on

May 6 for a rules interpretation meeting with Hubert Johnson from Detroit, presenting to all district commissioners. Johnson will supervise a demonstration of legal and illegal pitches which has been a hot topic the previous year. Leo Fisher, ASA president, and M. J. Pauley, ASA secretary attended also. Pauley stated, "Softball can never be a successful pro sport as it is a recreational game." He finished by adding there are 40 states in the ASA and 145,000 member teams.

Whitmore told the enthusiastic crowd that the association expects 20,000 members this year compared to 700 in the inaugural 1934 season. This will result in the expansion of the district tournaments from 32 teams last year to 64 teams for the 1936 season. The state tournament will once again take place in Lansing from September 4 – 7. Whitmore added that there would be a reduction of districts in Michigan from 18 to 16.

The state decided to retain the 10th man on teams by a vote of 13-3. The biggest reason is it would not allow as many players as possible to participate. The state also set up two classes of play; an A and B division.

On July 15 it was announced that it was estimated 90 teams would play in this year's state tournament in Lansing. The City has four lighted fields and another ten hard clay diamonds. Teams must be sanctioned by the state by August 1 and district play must be finished by August 30. There are 320 teams eligible for district play. On August 14, Whitmore announced that fifteen districts will conduct tournaments to determine who will be competing in the state tournament and must be completed by August 30. Most of these will be held in cities who have lighted fields. The women's teams will not enter district tournaments, but must file their entries in the state tournament by August 20.

The state tournament for the women's team was set at 29 teams in two classes; A and B, with an upper and lower bracket in each class, which is different from the one class of play in 1935. There will be thirteen teams in the class A and sixteen teams in the class B. After district play ended for the men's teams, a total of forty-four teams will compete for the title in two separate classes similar to the women's tournament. Lansing Oldsmobile, last year's champion and Vaughan Battery of Lansing, last year's runner-up will return this year.

1936 State Tournament

After the first round of play on September 4, heavily favored Vaughan Battery of Lansing could only get two hits of Estil Tessmer of the Ann Arbor Gauss team and were eliminated 5-1. Lansing Oldsmobile defeated Frank Ferrell's of Grand Rapids, 3-0, behind a two-hit performance by outstanding pitcher Archie Tarpoff. The Oldsmobile team could only get two hits also, but poor fielding by the Frank Ferrell team cost them a win.

The women's first round ended with no real upsets, however, four Flint teams advanced into the second round and three more have yet to play because of stoppage from heavy rains. Heavily favored Kresges from Grand Rapids had their bats working as they overpowered Pohl Brothers from St. Johns 40-4. Three Lansing teams in Class A went down to defeat in the opening round.

Heavy rains continued into Sunday which delayed the start of second round games, but stopped long enough to allow play to resume before ending play in the early evening. It was feared that an extra day may have to be added as only eleven games were played. Another favorite, Saginaw Standard and Proos Plumbing of Grand Rapids were tied 2-2 after seven inning and will have to finish their game on Monday. That ended in a 5-4 win by the Grand Rapids team.

Protests of two games was the topic when play resumed on Monday. Twenty-seven games were scheduled with a 9:00 a.m. start which will push games into midnight with some teams forced to play three games. The Muskegon Campbell Wynant Cannon team walked off the field Sunday night after the team thought too many illegal pitches were called against them. They would resume play Monday on orders by tournament officials with the score at 6-0 for Oldsmobile Lansing. It was decided to use Saginaw umpires to finish the game which eventually ended with a 10-0 score. The committee decided to use outside umpires when Lansing teams were involved with teams from other districts. Players from the Royal Oak Romey Drugs team cried, "frame up" as they left the field in the sixth inning, behind 3-0 to Lansing Oldsmobile as they felt too many illegal pitches were being called unfairly. It was officially recorded as a 9-0 victory due to a forfeit.

Only one Woman's game was able to be played Sunday night as Ionia Friar's Ale won 9-4 over Lansing Michigan Company. Late Monday the quarter finals and semi-finals were completed to determine who would play at 7:00 p.m. Tuesday at Ranney Park for the championship. The Ann Arbor Silver Wings had to defeat Flint A.C. 8 to 3, then eliminated the fanored Kresge team from Grand Rapids, 13 – 2 in the semi-finals. They will play the Ionia Friar's Ale team which eliminated Benton Harbor Twin City Motor Coach, 7-1. The class A championship game will feature Vans of Lansing versus City Transport of Lansing.

The men's quarter-finals and semi-finals were also finished with finalists determined in each class. In class A, Lansing Oldsmobile will get a chance to defend their title after getting a forfeit win against Royal Oak Romey. They will face St. Joseph Auto Specialties who edged Ann Arbor Gauss, 2-1. The Class B finalist were Muskegon Weeks who barely beat a strong Coldwater team 2-1 and Lansing Secretary of State who beat Grand Rapids Millers 3-2.

Over 7,500 fans showed up Tuesday evening to watch the four championship games. In the women's class B, the Friars of Ionia outlasted the Ann Arbor Silver Wings 15-12 in a slug fest. The City Transport team from Lansing in class AT retained their title with a 4-3 win over Vans, another Lansing team. The Secretary of State team of Lansing shutout Weeks of Muskegon 5-0 behind the four-hit pitching of Harry Monson to win the men's class B title. The feature game of the evening saw the Auto Specialties team from Ann Arbor upset the defending champs, Lansing Oldsmobile 1 to 0. The game took less than an hour to play.

The four champions will represent Michigan in the national softball tournament in Chicago September 12-14. Unfortunately no record could be found of how the Michigan teams did, but Briggs team from Detroit won the title in 1937.

Michigan champions in 1937 and 1938 were the women's team, Lansing Vans. St. Joe Autos won the men's Major championship four out of the first six years and also won 127 games while losing only 13 in 1937-38. Their schedules included teams from Indiana, Wisconsin, Illinois, Ohio and Kentucky. The little town of Woodland, with approximately 400 citizens, drew over 4,000 spectators in 1938, with its lighted park for the Barry county playoffs.

By 1939, the publication "Softball" was started in Lansing, Michigan by the Michigan ASA. Seth Whitmore of Lansing was the original editor and sponsor of the newspaper. The newspaper sold for ten cents, yearly subscription was 75 cents and had an average circulation of 6,100 readers.

Ball game in the Green Lake Field House gym, Green Lake neighborhood, Seattle, 1933 or 1934. (Image courtesy of the University of Washington Library Digital Collections.)

Photo of Subscription Ad for Softball Magazine

CHAPTER FOUR

WORLD WAR II BEGINS, ASA, AND MSA BARELY AFFECTED

The events of WWII are important to describe to fully understand the enormous impact the war had on America and the sport of softball as it relates to ASA and MSA.

1938

The world was involved in a war since 1938 although the actual "first shot" didn't occur until the invasion of Poland in 1939. when Europe and the Pacific countries were under attack. European countries began falling like dominoes as Adolf Hitler and the Nazis were taking over. Austria was the first to be taken by Germany when troop marched into the country, ousted Austrian chancellor Kurt Schuschnigg was placed under house arrest. and the annexation occurred on March 12, 1938. This was announced on the Heldenplatz in Vienna.

The Emperor of Japan, Showa, better known as Hirohito, who has been ruler since 1926, is also taking over countries and islands in the Pacific Ocean. The invasion of China took place in early 1938 and would continue through most of the year.

Adolf Hitler wanted to annex more land from surrounding countries to rebuild Germany from what was taken from them at the end of WWI. Called the Sudentenland, Hitler was determined to look at Czechoslovokia next. Nevelle Chamberlain, prime minister of England urged the leaders to make concessions to Hitler. On May 28, 1938 Germany had 96 divisions on the border ready for an invasion.

Hitler announced that Jews could no longer own businesses but could rent and soon he would exclude them from holding commercial or industrial jobs.

Concentration camps were being built secretly. Germany was pouring money and using citizens to build up the air force, navy with U-boats and battleships, and an enormous amount of armored tanks. It became increasingly obvious what Hitler was up to and leaders in England and France realized there was basically no way to stop Hitler's determination to annex more land.

June saw over 1,500 Jews sent to concentration camps and Hitler was assured by intelligence that England would do nothing if Czechoslovakia was invaded. On July 15, England, France, the United States and 26 other countries met in France to discuss the issue of Jews fleeing Germany. Nothing came from this meeting to solve the problem, in fact England and the United States refuses to accept any more Jewish refugees. In September, Winston Churchill could not convince parliament to allow Czechoslovakia to be protected and Franklin Roosevelt announce the United

States would remain neutral.

On September 27, president Roosevelt sends a letter to German Fuhrer, Adolf Hitler seeking peace. Pope Pius sent letters to Hitler during the war also, calling him "friend". The Munich Agreement, allowing Germany to annex Czechoslovakia Sudetenland in exchange for peace was signed by Germany, France England, and Italy three days later. This attempt to appease Hitler would fail again and again.

Germany invalidates the passports of all it Jewish citizens on October 5, by reissuing passports with the letter "J" stamped in red. This was done because of a request by Sweden and Switzerland as an easy way to deny Jews entry into their countries. The Jewish people were quickly losing their freedoms and their escape to countries for assistance and refuge.

Many European countries were also affected by the Great Depression but because of the war, employment began to rise as the need to build up the military became a necessity. especially in such countries as England and France. It is becoming obvious in the United States that the need to supply arms and equipment to England and France is a necessity, in hopes of staying out of the war. America would also begin building war ships, guns, planes, and equipment as experts were saying Japan would certainly attack us soon.

As the year draws to a close an important discovery is made; uranium fussion and physicists begin to study nuclear physics.

Leo Szilard, a Hungarian Physicist, that it was possible to develop a nuclear bomb and deduced that Germany was already doing research on such an idea.

ASA

How did World War II affect softball and ASA? As many other organizations suffered, softball under the direction and wisdom of ASA actually flourished, especially in the military. President Wilber Landis' foresight played a major role in the development of the Briggs Beautyware Company, which won national fast pitch titles in 1937, '48. '52 and '53. He convinced Briggs that softball would be a morale booster and soon other industrial companies would follow suit.

In 1928, Landis joined the Industrial Relations Division of Detroit Briggs Manufacturing Company and the company sponsored athletic programs. By the mid-1940's the program expanded to 400 bowling teams, 100 softball teams, and numerous other sports such as; baseball, golf, tennis, basketball and other sports. In 1934, Landis organized the Industrial Association of Detroit which eventually would have more than thirty-seven industrial firms, representing 210,000 Motor City workers.

Members of that association would form inter-city competition in softball, golf, boxing, basketball, hockey, tennis, and other team sports. During the war years this organization would play a major role in keeping softball "alive" and also see another avenue for ASA growth.

Industrial softball wasn't an invention of Landis, he just saw the advantages of playing sports during and after work. Way back in 1914, Eastman Kodak of Rochester, New York, would have softball games for three leagues during every lunch hour, five days a week. Those games started at 12:30 pm and lasted exactly 30 minutes. Uniforms could not be worn, because there wasn't time to change from work clothes to uniforms.

As the public began clamoring for more offense because of the windmill delivery, ASA decided that bunting should be permitted. Also, pitchers whose teams wore light gray or white uniforms were now required to wear a contrasting color.

During the year, 1938, women's softball was played at Madison Square Garden, called the Metropolitan Women's Softball League. There are photos of the New York Roverettes and the Americanettes with Babe Ruth taken. Other teams in the league were: Sheridan Park, Manhattan Beach, Brooklyn Rangers, and New Jersey Poppy Mills. Their uniforms were bright, interesting, and quite flashy, being made of colorful satin fabrics. Most women's teams wore shorts, although more conservative communities had women in pants. Bi-weekly games were played in Madison Square Garden by the Roverettes against teams from all over the country and Canada. An actual scorecard of a game between the Roverettes and the *Toronto Langley-Lakesides* exists but the photo of it is not clear enough for display in this book.

Photo of poster of games between teams.

The official newsletter, "Softball In Michigan", debuted in May and would later be named just "SOFTBALL", and would become an international publication. ASA's "Balls and Strikes" would stop publishing in June of 1942 before resuming in 1947.

1939

Timeline of Important WWII Events

- January 6 – Lise Meitner, a Jewish woman from Vienna publishes her discovery known as the "atom splitting" during her exile in Sweden.

- January 20 – Adolf Hitler proclaims his intention to parliament to exterminate all European Jews.

- January 25 – Enrico Fermi takes part in the first nuclear fission experiment. The splitting of a uranium atom, with John R. Dunning and Herbert Anderson.

- January 30 - Hitler threatens all European Jews by stating if International Jewish financiers lead the world into another war they will be annihilated.

- February 6 – The Spanish government flees to France. Francisco Franco is now the Spanish general ruling Spain.

- February 14 – The German battleship "Bismarck" is launched in Hamburg.

- February 24 – The anti-Communist pact is signed by Hungary with Germany, Italy and Japan.

- March 16 – Germany occupies the rest of Czechoslovakia and Hitler delivers his famous words, "Czechoslovakia has ceased to exist."

- March 28 – Poland formally rejects Hitler's demand that

Danzig is ceded to Germany.

- March 31 – England and France agree to support Poland in the event of a German invasion.

- April 1 – Following the end of the Spanish Civil War, the United States recognizes the Franco government in Spain.

- April 8 – By order of Benito Mussolini, Italy seizes the country of Albania.

- April 19 – England announces it will defend Denmark, the Netherlands and Switzerland in the event of a war.

- April 20 – Russian leader Joseph Stalin signs the British-France-Russian anti-German pact.

- May 4 – Japanese Prime Minister, Kiichiro Hiranuma, declares Japan will support Germany and Italy in the event of an attack, but not immediately.

- May 11 – Outer Mongolia is attacked by the Japanese army.

- May 22 – Germany and Italy sign the "pact of steel" committing them to a military alliance.

- May 27 – The SS St. Louis sails into Havana, Cuba with over 900 Jewish refugees fleeing the Nazis but they are turned away and refused refuge.

- June 4 – The SS St. Louis is denied permission to land in Florida.

- July 3 – Ernst Heinkel, German aircraft designer,

demonstrates an 800 kph rocket plane to Hitler.

- July 6 – Hitler closes down the last Jewish enterprises and businesses.

- July 28 – Fighting on the Manchurian border finally ceases between Russia and Japanese troops.

- August 2 – Albert Einstein writes president Roosevelt about using uranium to develop an atomic bomb.

- August 24 – Germany and the USSR sign a 10-year non-aggression pact.

- August 30 – Poland begins to mobilize to defend itself from a possible German attack.

- August 31 – Nazis dressed as Poles stage an assault on a radio station in Gleiwitz as an excuse to invade Poland.

- September 1 – Poland is invaded by the German "Blitzkrieg" by attacking the city of Danzig. Hitler also initiates the T4 Euthanasia Program, ordering the extermination of the mentally ill.

- September 3 – England, France, Australia, New Zealand, South Africa and

- Canada declare war on Germany.

- September 4 – The Netherlands and Belgium declare neutrality.

- September 6 – The first German air attack on England

begins.

- September 21 – Nazi leader, Reinhard Heydrich, meets in Berlin to discuss the "final solution" of Jews.

- September 27 – After 19 days of resistance, Warsaw surrenders to the Germans. This was precipitated by German Luftwaffe fire bomb strikes.

- October 6 – Hitler denies he intends to go to war with England and France.

- October 14 – German U-47 sinks the British battleship, HMS Royal Oak and 833 seamen perish.

- October 24 – Hitler orders Jews to wear the Star of David to be recognized and segregated.

- October 26 – Hitler forces Polish Jews into obligatory work or slave labor.

- October 30 – Germany and the USSR agree on partitioning Poland and Hitler begins to deport Jews.

- November 4 – The U.S. Congress authorizes "cash and carry" arms sales to help France and England.

- November 8 – A failed assassination attempt on Hitler is made in Munich.

- November 15 – Mass anti-German demonstrations break out in Czechoslovakia. Nazis begin the mass murder of Warsaw Jews.

- November 30 – The Russo-Finnish war begins as Stalin orders an attack with 540,000 men and 2,486 tanks. Helsinki is bombed.

- December 14 – After the 105-day Russo-Finnish war, the League of Nations expels the Soviet Union for invading Finland.

- December 18 – Off the coast of Uruguay, the German battleship, "Graf Spee" is scuttled by its crew members as they were trapped by British cruisers.

- December 21 – Hitler names Adolf Eichmann, a high ranking Nazi SS officer to be in charge of evictions and Jewish immigration.

ASA

During its early years, some people doubted the success of ASA. In the inaugural January issue of "Softball", editor Seth Whitmore wrote, "The effort of a few to discredit the ASA failed. At the National AAU convention the executive board of that body voted unanimously to continue the alliance with the ASA and lauded our association for its record." The National Y.M.C.A. softball committee voted at its annual meeting in Chicago to continue its full cooperation with the ASA.

The American Softball Association, a professional league run by George Sisler, recognized the ASA as the governing body of softball. Seth Whitmore wrote in his column, "Softball Servings", "There is every indication that friction will be at a very minimum in 1940 and organized softball will march forward to greater peaks than any previously reached."

At its annual meeting, Leo Fischer was re-elected as president and Walter Hakanson was elected vice president, succeeding Early Maxwell of Memphis, Tennessee. M.J. Pauley was once again re-elected to the post of executive secretary. Pauley stated, "There is no such thing as an exhibition game in his opinion. A softball game is a game and no player should be permitted to play with other than his own team in any game. Adding players of other teams for games is a sin against all amateur rules.

The ASA announced it would be publishing a newsletter dedicated to further the enhancement of amateur softball. It will be called Balls and Strikes. The ASA was criticized by the National AAU for allowing Joe Louis to compete as an amateur in softball. ASA apologized because our book clearly states, "by earning a livelihood from any position where athletic skill is the principal requirements of his or her employment.

It was announced that the 1939 softball guide and rule book would be published about March 15, for distribution. ASA representative, Dudley Stilton, in England announced that there would be a softball season this summer for 24 teams after the entire season was down last year due to unfavorable weather. A lengthy article was posted in Balls and Strikes on how to organize a softball league and Judge Kenesaw Mountain Landis, commissioner for Major League Baseball emphasized that softball isn't a danger to the great sport of baseball but rather helps the sport as any outdoor sport is good for the game.

In reference to women's softball, ASA stated, "After WWI, the bloomer girls passed into history, but in the late 20's there was a renewal of interest in softball, and when the women came out to play a modern version of the bloomer, middie blouse and tennis shoes constituted their uniform. As time passed bloomers and middies gave way to trunks and a more stylish blouse that enabled a free arm swing. Although trunks predominate in most sections of the country today, the modern miss in softball wears a uniform that is similar to those worn by baseball players. They also eliminate mush of the danger of injury in sliding. Many teams wear sliding pads, while this year catchers must wear body protectors under the new rules and masks are also required.

It was once said that girl's softball drew the crowds because of the novelty, and the 'leg show'. However, the novelty has worn off, girls no longer appear as a chorus, and the crowds are larger than ever. The fact is that members of the fair sex, playing a fast and skillful game today, offer more entertainment for followers of the sport and the future for them has never been brighter."

ASA announced a "moving picture" on a 16 m.m. reel will be available through the national office in either silent or sound. The only requirement is that postage be paid to and from Chicago.

The picture was made by the Briggs Manufacturing Company and is the first of its kind in Softball. Within a month the requests were so large, that the supply of films ran out and more needed to be produced.

According to Puerto Rico softball commissioner, Mr. R. Sontiago Sosa, he had hopes that Puerto Rico would have their champion competing in the World Softball Championship. Evaristo Prado of Havana, Cuba, stated that softball is taking the country by storm and are thinking of the idea of promoting a Havana championship in the very near future.

On May 9th a special doubleheader was held at Madison Square Garden in New York City to open their softball season. Over 15,000 fans paid $5.00 each to attend and cheer on their favorite players and teams. The Langley Lakesides women's teams from Toronto, Canada, behind the pitching of Thelma Golden who struck out twelve, beat the famed Roverettes of New York, 3 to 1, while the famed men's team of Lowell Thomas, "Nine Old Men" tromping the Thomas Ripley team, "Believe it or Nots" by a possible score of 77-10. A colossal home run by the famed Babe Ruth was the highlight of the game as the ball reached the upper deck of the Garden. Other's on Ripley's team were; Walter Johnson, Jack White, Gene Tunney, and Jack Dempsey along with about 20 other dignitaries. Both teams wore very outlandish colorful uniforms with the "Nine Old Men" wearing straw hats instead of ball caps, while the "Believe it or Nots" team wore bright red Arabian turbans wrapped around their heads.

The month of May also saw the formation of a national association of umpires called; Amateur Softball Association of America Officials Association and will be handled by the ASA national office. Dues will be $2.00 per year which will go towards an official insignia on the cap, a membership card, a year's subscription to "SOFTBALL" and a copy of the Official Guide and rule book of the ASA. In addition officials will receive bulletins on rules interpretations and they can also write the national office for rulings. By July, numerous states stated umpire enthusiasm to join.

Dudley Shumway, commissioner of California announced that a softball Jamboree" would be held at the Los Angeles Memorial Coliseum on June 30. There will be six games going on at once from 6 pm to 11 pm and an estimated 60,000 will be sold for the event.

The Veterans of Foreign Wars (VFW) has requested assistance from the ASA to help promote their own Junior World's Championships (17 and under). The national office of ASA ask that all commissioners do everything they can to assist the VFW. It was later announced that the tournament will take place in Bessemer, Alabama sometime in August. A total of 30 teams filed entries as of July.

M. J. Pawley, executive secretary of the ASA, pointed out the need to include more women in leadership roles and declared he was in favor of working toward the day when the game will have women managers and coaches on the field. He also urged commissioners to work diligently to get more women and girls to attend softball meetings. Mrs. H. R. Harvey of Lansing spoke and stated this, "No other summer sport appeals to so many girls physically. Recommendations for girls teams might be: 1. Every girl playing before a crowd should be sixteen years of age. 2. Every girl should have a physical examination before playing. 3. Men coaches are allowable, but there should be a woman manager with each team. 4. Girls should be used for coaching the bases."

It was officially announced that the World's Softball Championships will be held in Chicago from September 6 to 12. The champions will be decided in Soldier Field. Tens of thousands of teams will be competing during the month of August to represent their states, cities, and possibly even countries. Reports from everywhere indicate a greater interest in girls' softball this year which will increase the size of the tournament. Never before in history have so many persons competed in any one sport.

Due to the vast increase in teams playing in qualifying tournaments, the official softball factory is three weeks behind in deliveries. The ASA advised all states and municipalities to quickly get their orders in to avoid being without these softballs. Remember ALL TOURNAMENTS MUST use the official ASA softball.

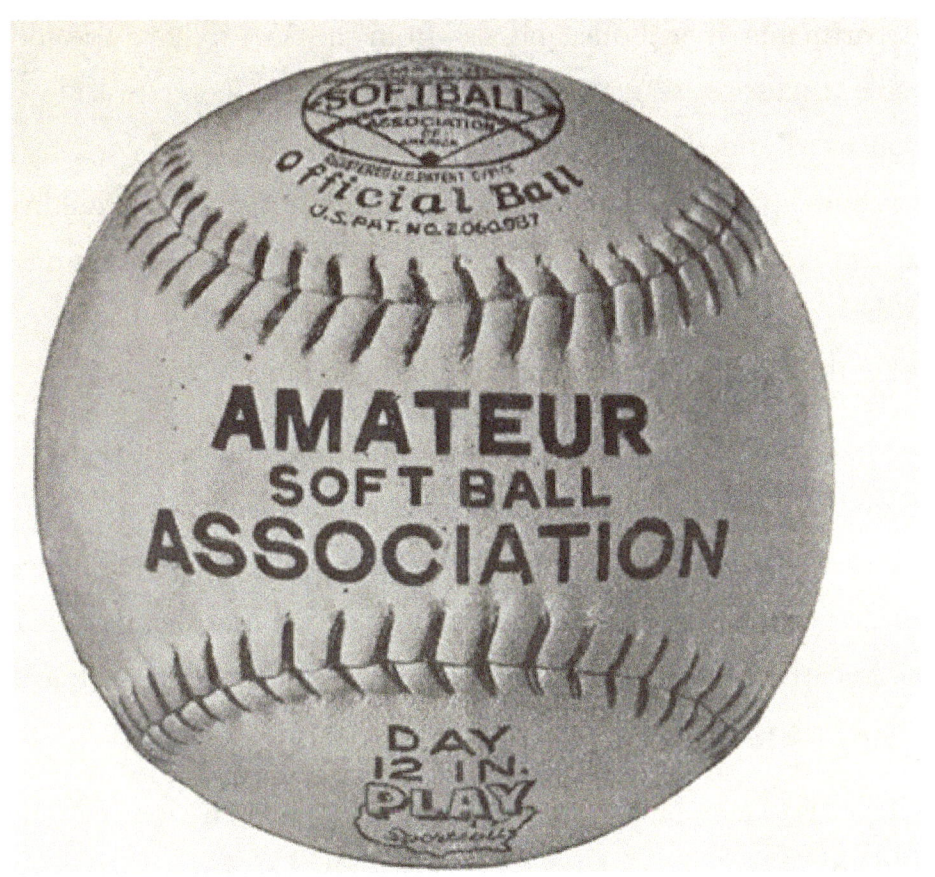

Photo of the Official ASA Softball

M. J. Pawley ruled that member teams of the ASA to cancel all games scheduled with the member teams of George Sisler's North and South Side parks of Chicago. The Sisler league teams have been temporarily suspended because they were discovered playing for cash prizes, which is in violation of amateur rules. Sisler is also president of the American Softball Association which is not affiliated with the Amateur Softball Association. A meeting was set up in St. Louis, Missouri with several key people from parks departments in St. Louis and also from the ASA to have a round table discussion to try and resolve the issue. George Sisler was contacted and the people waited from 3 pm to 6 pm for Sisler to show up and when no phone call occurred saying he wouldn't attend, the meeting was cancelled. Several teams representing Sisler's organization in St. Louis, Peoria, Illinois and Indianapolis were then also suspended along with their teams.

Miss Lorraine Gehrke, shortstop and captain of the Parichy Bloomer girls of Forest Park, Illinois is being referred to as the Lou Gehrig of softball. Only 22 years old, she is competing in her ninth year and has not missed one game! She has played in 441 consecutive games and 3,290 consecutive innings. Playing almost all positions, she has compiled a lifetime average of .325.

Chet Ternacki, pitcher for the Bendix Air Brakes of South Bend, Indiana, has won 96 games and lost only 10 in the past three years. In 1935 he pitched the Toledo, Ohio, Crimson Coaches to a national title and led the Briggs Body team of Detroit to the same honor in 1937.

World Championships Underway

The seventh annual world's softball championships got underway at Soldier field on Thursday, September 7, with a parade of teams, opening ceremonies, and two outstanding games played that evening. Ninety teams representing more than 40 states, three Canadian provinces, and Puerto Rico are entered this year. Defending champions, Alameda, California women's team and

Pohlar Café, men's team from Cincinnati, will be competing also. On Friday and Saturday, six different parks will be used for play with Soldier Field set for Championship play on September 11. Tournament officials are hoping for better weather this year as rain held up numerous games in 1938.

After six days of great softball the men's team of Nick Carr Boosters from Covington, Kentucky beat Ferguson State Auditor of Columbus, Ohio, 5 to 1 for title. Norb "the Cyclone" Warken was 6 – 0 with five shutouts, two no-hitters, and 14 strikeouts in the championship game. Amazingly he didn't allow a walk in 52 innings pitched. In the eleven games he pitched to win the Kentucky state and world title, Walkin had nine shutouts and 161 strikeouts.

Other notable pitchers were: Ralph Solt, Ferguson, tossed three consecutive no-hitters, shutting out Briggs, Detroit 1-0 in eleven innings to win the semi-final game. Diz Kirkendall threw two no-hitters for Pohlar's Café of Cincinnati. One was a 1 – 0 loss to Columbus which eliminated his team. Most Valuable Player of the tournament was Warken.

JJ Kriegs Haberdashers, of Alameda, California, defended their title by beating Kentucky Dairy Maids from Louisville, with a no-hit 1-0 win. They won all five games by scores of 5-2, 14-0, 6-5, 1-0 and 1-0. They won the semi-final game over Pony Express Team from St. Joseph, Missouri, 1-0 in 12 innings. Bessie Johnson pitched all ten games in the last two tournaments and it was reported the Kriegs team won 102 games in a row the past two years.

It should be noted that fourteen year old Virginia Fraburt defeated the Arizona Ramblers 2-1 and star hurler, Louise Curtis Miller in the semi-finals before only giving up three hits in the loss to Kriegs. The Ramblers finished third for the third consecutive year. The unofficial MVP was Bessie Johnson who also had a hit in the championship game.

During a meeting on September 9, 1939, at the Morrison Hotel in Chicago, the ASA showed a deficit of only $621.36, money owed Pauley, who had been elected secretary-treasurer for the seventh consecutive term. A resolution commending Walter O. Briggs of the Briggs Manufacturing Company, for the wonderful work his team, Briggs Beautyware, did for softball during the 1938 season was adopted at the annual meeting of the commissioner's council of the ASA.

Note: Later in the year Leo Fischer resigned as president because he though the ASA was being used for the promotion of a commercial product. This will be covered in the following chapter.

Michigan Softball Association

Seth Whitmore discontinued the Softball of Michigan newsletter after four years and in January, announced the debut of "Softball" which will be published by the Michigan Softball Association.

He wrote on the front page: SOFTBALL, Becomes First Official Publication. He wrote, "We are not starting on such an extensive scale that our resources will become exhausted with the second or third issues. On the contrary we are starting at the bottom with a publication that has unlimited possibilities in serving those who play, sponsor and enjoy softball."

He added, "Like any other publication we must devote the greatest measure of space to the territory in which we have the highest circulation. More than 5,000 copies of this issue are being distributed in every state, in Canada, the Philippines and elsewhere. Unlike previous softball publications, Softball has no salaried executives, no stockholders, and no expensive office overhead. We welcome suggestions, stories and unusual pictures from anyone interested in the progress of softball as a clean, wholesome, amateur recreation. This is your paper. It will be what you make it. Only through your cooperation can we succeed."

On page 2, Whitmore editorialized by saying, "Softball grew up in the depression and has won its way into the daily life of millions. It is a great amateur sport and its future is bright. We still have millions of unemployed. One third of the nation is in poverty. To these people softball other recreation, free or at a very low cost, is of unestimatible value. However, softball, as an established pastime today has permanent fans in all walks of life."

Whitmore ended by saying, "American people are sport conscious. While the masses in Europe are crushed under the feet of dictators, and little children don't know what it is to smile, the millions in America turn out daily to witness games of football, baseball, softball, basketball, and other great sports. A nation that has learned to cheer and play the game as we have on the diamond and gridiron is not fertile soil for a Hitler."

During these winter months sports enthusiasts are finding that ice skating on flood lighted rinks is allowed because of lighting softball facilities. One of the chief arguments presented to municipalities by groups seeking lights for softball is the fact that parks can be flooded for the use of two sports. Hoyt Park, in Saginaw, is a natural "bowl" with 6 softball fields and is flooded each winter for ice skating. It also has a warming house.

The Auto Specialties Manufacturing team from St. Joseph, Michigan's major champs in 1936, 1937, and 1938, established a state record without equal. During the '38 season, they played 66 games, winning 59, scoring 271 runs while holding their opponents to just 45 runs. Forty-four of those wins were shutouts, and in seven games they only allowed one run. The outstanding pitching staff; Ray Kaczmarek, Earl Flamme, and Dave Green combined for 848 strikeouts and seven no-hitters. The team had only one run scored against them in three state championship tournaments, and that was in the very first game in 1936. Quite an accomplishment.

A severe disability didn't stop Calumet Journal Newsboys teammate, Bobby Giroux, 17, from becoming an outstanding pitcher. With two badly crippled arms, and only four fingers on each hand, he was given special permission to pitch as legally as possible. He struck out more batters than any pitcher in the league and in one game fanned sixteen batters, while allowing only one hit. He also enjoys playing hockey, tennis and basketball.

The annual MSA business meeting was held in Lansing and drew a total of 55 delegates, the largest attendance in history. One of the biggest issues discussed was the dominance of pitching in the fast pitch game, the banning of metal cleats, removing the tenth man, and moving back the pitching distance. There is a news clipping of a pitcher tossing his fifty-second no-hitter last fall. There is a real problem when a pitcher can achieve that.

Photo or Ad for solid rubber cleats

A majority of the membership voted to eliminate the tenth player by a vote of 130-82, and the pitching distance be moved from 40 feet to 45 feet by a vote of 134-75. The membership requested that the new rules be given a fair trial and another statewide vote be taken on July 1 of this year. The banning of metal cleats was passed by a 177-42 vote.

In May, "Rudy" Schmeling, the Saginaw district commissioner, who reported 120 teams in his area last year, submitted more than twice as many memberships as any other area despite having eight counties eliminated from his large district. Three leagues, American, National, and Merchants are already set for play in Saginaw. Organization of the Northeastern Michigan league has been completed with ten teams; Bennett Field, Owosso, Monarch Service and Graebner Dairy from Saginaw, Alma, St. Louis, Caro, Sebewaing, the Bay City Elks, Harold's tavern from Reese and the Clare Merchants.

The VanDervoort women's team of Lansing, major champions in 1937 and 1938 announced they will travel extensively this year. They have scheduled games in Toronto, Chicago, Buffalo, Detroit and several other cities. They also hope to play a couple of games in Madison Square Garden.

A regional tournament will be held in Lansing on July 28-30 with eight men's teams and four women's teams competing. They will come from Ohio, Indiana, and Michigan along with metropolitan districts of Detroit, Cleveland and Cincinnati. Detroit will conduct a special tournament to decide who will represent their district while Michigan will conduct a major playoff between Garber Buick, Saginaw, McKinnon Mooney, Flint, Oldbru, Ann

Arbor, Fitzgerald Club, Grand Ledge, Big Six, Pontiac, and Shaw's, Pontiac to represent Michigan. Neutral umpires will be provided for all games. Vandervoort from Lansing will represent Michigan in the women's regional joining teams from Detroit, Cleveland and Cincinnati. Tickets will be priced at 25 cents for adults and 10 cents for children.

Photo of men's and women's champions.

The city of Lansing now boasts of four lighted facilities which can seat nearly 10,000 spectators and yearly attendance is estimated at 400,000. In observance of the tenth anniversary of the launching of softball at Ranney park, the recreation department will be hosting the regional tournament.

The Upper Peninsula is becoming a real hotbed for softball and its estimated that over 400 teams play there. Following meetings at Negaunee and Sault Ste. Marie, state commissioner Seth Whitmore decided that it would be best for the U.P. to be set up into six regions and in 1940 to hold tournaments in each region. Due to time restrictions it was decided that only one tournament would be held this year.

Detroit's department of recreation directors Hubert Johnson and John Schierlinger announced that 51,000 softball players are participating on 3,400 teams. They said only 366 baseball teams have 6,588 players, which give softball an 8-1 numerical edge over "America's pastime". There are 214 softball diamonds in the city and they are in such demand that five permits for each park every day are in demand. This allows teams to play virtually from 10 a.m. until dark, and the recreation departments are having a difficult time meeting the demands.

A total of thirty cities will host district and sub-district tournaments to determine teams that will compete in state tournament play in Lansing on September 1-5. The classification of teams was causing a real problem, as many A teams want to play in the B classification and numerous B teams want to be classified as C teams.

The major tournament, spread over three weeks ended with Big Six, Pontiac and Oldbru, Ann Arbor being the Michigan representatives in the central regional tournament, also known as the Tri-State Tournament. ASA is hoping the success of this tournament and the one held in Washington, D.C., that it will be adopted on a national scale in 1940. Then regional winners would compete in a world's tournament with a two game knockout basis.

When the Tri-State Regional tournament ended on July 30 the women's team, Erin Brew from Cleveland, were crowned champions. Jerry Joyce, the ace hurler tossed successive no-hit, no run games as they defeated Pfeiffers of Ann Arbor, 6-1 and 9-0 before besting Romans of Detroit 3-0 in the championship game.

Champions of Central Region

Photo by Irwin Hinchey

Smiling over their newly won championship, the Erin Brew girls of Cleveland, metropolitan champions of that city, are shown above as they gathered for a picture after winning the Central regional championship in a Tri-State tournament at Lansing. They defeated Pfeiffer's of Ann Arbor 6 to 1 and 9 to 0 and the Romans of Detroit 3 to 0 to gain the title. They were the only team to go through the meet undefeated. Bernice "Jerry" Joyce, center of bottom row, pitched all three games, turning in successive no-run, no-hit victories over Ann Arbor and Detroit to become the individual girl star of the tournament.

Photo of Erin Brew Women's team.

The Big Six team from Pontiac, already recognized as the world's Negro softball champions, were the men's champions after winning five of six games. Behind the pitching of Charles Justice and Elijah Burt, they dominated in the five games won. They had to face Hudson Motors from Detroit in the championship game, the only team to beat them earlier in the tournament, 3-1. Hudson took the lead in the championship game when Ted Bankey homered over the right field fence in the fifth inning to give his team a 2-1 lead. However, in the sixth inning, three runs scored by Big

Six when Ruby Taylor singled, King walked, and Justice was safe on a fielder's choice and an error drove in Taylor. Hooper singled scoring King and Justice came home after an outfield fly. Hudson Motors was held scoreless in the seventh inning to give Big Six the victory.

In the September issue of "Softball", editor Whitmore stated, "in the past few years, records show that while softball has recruited an even greater army of players, men over 30 years of age are dropping out of the game. It has become too fast, especially in the class where pitchers constitute 80 percent of the game."

"Some say the answer to this is to slow the game down, move the pitcher back or something else. We do not believe any of these suggested changes will help. What we need is the promotion and development of slow pitching softball, which, when given a chance, has progressed rapidly. In the slow pitch game, there is plenty of speed and action and the pitcher does not prevent other members of the team from participating in the fun."

"We don't know what rule changes will be made this fall, but we believe we are safe in predicting that if the pitcher continues to dominate the game as he is today, the slow pitching game, in a very short time, will succeed the faster game."

Winners of the state tournaments were: Men's Major: Big Six, Pontiac, A: Autos, St. Joseph, B: Midwest Refinery, Alma, C: Billiards, Chesaning, Women's Major: VanDervoort's, Lansing, A: Nehi, Jackson, B: Autos, St. Joseph, C: A. C., Flint.

1940

World War II Timeline of Events

- February 1 - The Soviet forces invade Finland with overwhelming troop and equipment numbers. They are faced with Finnish resistance.

- February 14/15 – Britain announces their merchant ships would be armed and the next day Germany announces that merchant ships would be classified as warships.

- March 13 – After five weeks of fighting, the "Treaty of Moscow" ends the invasion of Finland. Despite being outnumber 3:1 by forces, 30:1 by aircraft and 100:1 by tanks, the Finns had retained their sovereignty.

- April 9 – Germany invades Denmark and Norway.

- May 10 – Germany invades Holland, Belgium and Luxemburg. King George VI! appoints Winston Churchill as British Prime Minister, replacing Neville Chamberlain who constantly sought appeasement with Germany.

- May 11 – Churchill orders the bombing of Berlin, although having only three medium bombers able to take the war to Germany.

- May 12 – The ill-prepared French defenses at Sedan are overrun by German forces. Captured bridges would allow tanks and the army to pour across giving them direct access to the underdefended Allied frontline.

- May 24 – After days of movement by armored divisions, Hitler order the halt to allow infantry divisions to catch up so an assault could happen against Allied forces.

- May 26 – Operation Dynamo begins so a full scale evacuation of British and French troops trapped at Dunkirk could begin.

- June 4 – Using destroyers, large ships, and flotilla of about 700 small boats of all kinds, crewed by civilians helped evacuate more than 330,000 troops.

- June 7 – General Erwin Rommel's VII Panzer Divisions advances 37 miles in two days and the next day the last French lines of defense falls at Aisne and Somme.

- June 10 – Mussolini, Leader of Italy, declares war on France and Britain with the idea of expanding Italian colonies in British and French territories in North Africa.

- June 13 – French troops abandon Paris and German troops enter the city in the early hours of the next day. Panzer tanks would roll past the Arc de Triomphe, down the Champs Elysees to Place de la Concorde.

- June 17 – Marshal Petain broadcasts to the French people urging them to stop resisting while asking the Germans for the terms of an armistice.

- June 20 – Italy launches an offensive on the Alpine front with the intention of defeating what remains of French forces and take control of the Alps and the port of Nice on the Mediterranean Sea.

- June 22 – France surrenders and is split in two, the Germans control the north and the south becomes known as "Vichy France."

- July 16 – Hitler plans for the invasion of Britain (Operation Sealion). The objective is to land 160,000 troops in south-east Britain with air and naval supremacy in the English Channel.

- July 29 – Japanese Foreign Minister, Hachiro Arita announces Japans intention to establish a bloc of Asian nations led by the Japanese and free from Western powers.

- August 1 – Hitler orders that victory should be quick, with the obliteration of all RAF planes and ground support along with the total destruction of the entire British aircraft industry.

- August 5 – The Battle of Britain begins with nearly 3,000 German aircraft outnumbering the RAF by four to one.

- August 13 – On "Eagle Day", the German Luftwaffe launches 1,485 sorties against the RAF airfields. The RAF loses only 14 planes while the Luftwaffe suffers the loss of 45 planes.

- August 15 – Germany launches its most intense attack with over 1,000 aircraft and 1,750 sorties. The British airfields suffer major damage.

- August 24 – Central London is attacked for the first time as a lost formation of German bombers mistakenly drop their loads on the capital.

- August 25 – In retaliation, the RAF bomber command launches its first night attack on industrial targets around Berlin.

- September 3 – President Roosevelt signs the "Lend-Lease Agreement" with Britain in return for 50 WWI destroyers. Britain allows the U.S. a 99 year lease to several British and naval bases.

- September 7 – The Blitz of London begins with night-time raids by 600 planes. It was designed to lower the morale of the people but it allowed the rebuilding of the RAF airfields which had been close to defeat.

- September 13 – Italy invades Egypt.

- September 17 – After failing to take control of the skies over Britain, Hitler postpones "Operation Sealion" until further notice. He orders the dismissal of 2,000 barges held in Belgian, French and German harbors.

- September 22 – Japan occupies French Indochina.

- September 27 – The "Tripartite Pact (Axis) is signed in Berlin by Germany, Italy and Japan promising mutual aid.

- September 28 – The "Battle of Britain" ends with the Luftwaffe loses 1,400 aircraft to the RAF loses of 800 planes.

- October 12 – Hitler formally cancels "Operation Sealion" as he now focuses on the possible invasion of Russia.

- October 28 – Wanting to prove how strong Italy was, Mussolini orders the invasion of Greece.

- November 11 - The Royal Navy Fleet Air Arm attack the Italian navy at Taranto. In the first ever all aircraft naval battle, three battleships are sunk by torpedoes and bombs using obsolete British biplanes. The Japanese study this at is already preparing for an attack on Pearl Harbor.

- November 14 – In a massive air raid, 500 enemy aircraft attack the cities in the middle of Britain. The city of Coventry is all but destroyed by the use of incendiary bombs.

- November 15 – The Soviet Union is invited to join the Tripartite Pact and to share in the spoils of the British Empire.

- November 22 – The Italian IX army is defeated by the Greeks at Koritsa.

- November 25 – After Romania and Hungary sign the

Tripartite Pact, Soviet Union gives their terms if they join also, including new territorial gains.

- December 8 – Francisco Franco of Spain rules out their entry into the war, with the immediate result having Hitler canceling an attack on Gibralter.

- December 11 – Retreating Italian troops fleeing from captured Sidi Barrani, are easy targets for the British Royal Navy.

ASA

There were many states associated with ASA who have shown the growth of softball and the numerous parks with lighted fields. The use of the WPA funds allowed this to happen which helped the game of softball grow. The Great Depression is nearing an end as employment has gone up thanks to government programs and the buildup of our military equipment due to the assistance sent to England to help them fight the German attacks.

The February issue of "Balls and Strikes" mentioned the first book about softball is now on the market. It is called "Softball… So What?" by Lowell Thomas And Ted Shane. The article states, "Thomas and Shane have produced a unique and infectious American Opus that will make even an interior decorator want to go out and whacking the big apple. See it, buy it, and read it, you will laugh out loud, and you will be serious while leafing through it."

The ASA is struggling with numerous suspensions of players and teams as they want to travel around the country and try to make a living playing professional softball. Pauley urges these players and teams to remember ASA is an amateur organization and there is no "Pot of Gold" in softball as many large sponsors have found out. "We have no fight with professionalism.. If players think there is a lot of money in softball, let them find their own sponsors, lighted parks, and start Professional Softball."

Pauley adds, "And you, Mr. Sponsor, if a team asks your sponsorship and you would like to give it, we welcome you, and if any of the players on the teams asks for compensation for playing on your team tell them you want to sponsor an Amateur Team and not a Pro Team. You may not have the best team in the state in the first or second year, but you can take our word for it that you will have an outstanding team by the third year. No one wants to be a stool pigeon, but report to your own state or metropolitan commissioner any player who asks for money to play our game."

In another story in the newspaper is about nine Chicago women's players who thought they were worth "money" who were hiding behind the cloak of amateurism playing pro softball against amateur teams. They were called into the office of the Metropolitan Chicago commissioner and advised they would be suspended if it continued and were told in not so many words, "Nuts". Each and every player who participated in the now defunct Professional Indoor Baseball League this past winter are under amateur suspension.

The powerful Autos team from St. Joseph, Michigan has been a huge topic in that area of the country according to an article in the South Bend Tribune, by sports editor Jack Ledden, which has been closely observing the team since they entered baseball. The Autos won three state tournaments in Michigan, but just couldn't win a national tournament, and that is something Mr. Tiscornia couldn't tolerate. A sum of $12,000 is being expended by Mr. Tiscornia on a baseball park. Permanent seats for 3,000 will be provided and with plenty of empty seats, all he needs is a team that will win as consistently as his softball team did from 1936-1939.

Ledden stated, "The real reason is "new rules', which ASA has clarified by stating this spring a player must reside in the state in which he plays for six months. The Autos have been composed mostly by out of town men, from places such as; Illinois, Wisconsin, Cincinnati and Chicago. Thus its not hard to see that the rules and not Tiscornia, disbanded the Autos." Ledden finished by saying, "We wish Mr. Tiscornia enjoys success with his semi-pro baseball team and there is no personal objection to his shifting from one sport to another. If baseball doesn't pan out he can organize horseshoe pitching tournaments and still keep the dust in Edgewater park kicked up."

"The Spirit of American Youth" is the theme of the 1940 World's softball championship. From coast to coast on thousands of diamonds boys and girls are enjoying the sport, competing for district, regional, state, metropolitan and world's championships. While in most of the world youth is deprived of this opportunity under the regimentation of fascist and communist dictators. The war has stopped all softball activity in England for instance.

Dudley Stilton, softball commissioner for England for ASA, wrote M. J. Pauley the following letter, "I thank you very much for the Official softball guide book and as you may see from the above address, I am now in the Royal Air Force (RAF). Well they are exceptionally keen on sports and physical training here, so I think there is every chance of starting softball when the weather improves, unless of course our friend, the enemy, decides to start his military exercise. Then of course it will be a doubtful proposition."

Charles Johnson of Chicago was named this past summer to head the Amateur Softball Association Umpires Association, succeeding Harry Wilson. He is being assisted with rule interpretations by Hubert G. Johnson, Detroit, the official interpreter for the Joint Rules Committee on Softball as well as ASA.

Las Angeles will bid for the 1941 world's softball championships, according to Dudley Shumway, Southern California softball commissioner. Representatives of that city plan to attend the commissioners council meeting in Detroit to put in a bid. It is reported that two or three other cities outside of Detroit will also seek next year's championship event.

After seven years of Chicago hosting the World's Championship Tournament, it will be held in Detroit this year, from September 5 through 9. One hundred championship teams of men and women from practically every state, Canada and Puerto Rico will play in the largest amateur sport event on record. The opening ceremonies will take place in University of Detroit stadium on the night of September 5. The only states not participating were Nevada, Idaho and Oregon.

The first contest will be last year's champion from Covington, Kentucky against Detroit in the men's game and the champion from Alameda, California vs. Detroit in the women's contest. On September 6 and 7, games will take place at Northwestern Field and Belle Isle with the finals on September 9 at U. of D. stadium. Advance ticket sales indicate 50,000 spectators in the stadium alone with over 100,000 expected at the other two sites. Reserved seat prices are $1.10 for the finals, 75 cents for the semi-finals and 75 cents for opening night.

Several new rule changes will be instituted for this year's World Championship Tournament. The most important one is moving the pitching distance from 40 feet to 43 feet which is a compromise from those who wanted 45 feet and those wanting it to remain at 40 feet. Another change allows a batter to attempt to reach first base if the catcher doesn't catch a third strike.

The new wording of Section 1 of Rule 8 provides that the pitcher must stand with both feet squarely on the pitching plate for not less than one second before starting the delivery. The rule specifies that the one second may be determined by repeating at ordinary conversational speed the words, "One thousand and one". Section

8 Rule 3 has been changed so that the regulations requiring the pitcher's uniform to be of a dark solid color shall apply only when playing under lights.

Rule 3, Section 3 – Change in the configuration of home plate. It will be a five-sided figure square on the front and sides instead of the old diamond-shaped figure. Also Rule 4 – A note added to this rule makes it clear that no penalty affecting actual play can be imposed for the failure to report or announce an unreported substitution.

A very interesting article using somewhat humorous expressive words, was written by Warren Bornscheuer of the Baltimore Sun relating to softball. Titled: "Writer says Game is going Places". Although a little lengthy, it is too good not to be in this book. "For a sport that just cut its eyeteeth, softball is doing right well for itself. The first All-America game since lotto was invented, softball can be played with the skill of a Joe DiMaggio or the sluggishness of a Stepin Fetchit (Not an actual name). It is the new American Fever, the pastime of nearly 500,000 teams and 10 million players."

"Some will recall softball as a spineless form of baseball. It was called kitten ball, indoor baseball, sissy ball or dainty drawers, and it was played in the school yard years ago, It was safe and sane and was to baseball what beanbag-tossing was to bomb-throwing."

"This type of softball is still the tired old businessman's delight, but the real softballer will have no part of it. He plays a game that is as fast and furious as baseball. Streamlined softballers field and throw with tremendous 'oomph', run bases like Ty Cobb crossed with Steve Brodie."

"Down in Phoenix way around 1933, however, a lad named Paul Watson developed the knack of spinning his arm like a windmill, then releasing a lightning ball. At the same moment, a young man named John Baker , from Westport, Connecticut, developed a whirling-dervish, muddle-huddle movement which also ended with the release of a bullet-like projectile. This was known as the 'figure-8' windup and it was very mystifying indeed."

"The ball was thrown underhand, but with such speed the batter wasn't sure it had been pitched until he heard it plop into the mitt, behind him. And to make it tougher, these hurlers learned to put bewildering slants, hooks, and spins on the ball. The fielding and throwing and base-running also toughened, but it was the pitch that really drove the old softies too seek the company of their own kind."

"Without doubt, good hardball players can massacre the Nine Old Men type of play, but it takes a mighty skillful hardball team to beat a softball one. The reverse is not always true, softballers can often beat semi-pro teams at baseball."

It seems this writer knew what he was talking about when the mighty Babe Ruth couldn't see the ball during an exhibition game. He faced a farm boy named Hardy Brownwell, a fastball pitcher who threw three straight balls wide of the plate. Then, he reared back and unleashed a cannon ball over the plate which not only surprised Babe but also Lew Lehr, the catcher, who promptly left the game.

With another catcher in place, Brownwell threw another fireball which Babe swung at and missed. His next pitch, was a ball where Brownwell pulled the string at and humbled the "Sultan of Swat". The mighty Babe admitted he struck out because he couldn't see the ball. Just to convince himself and the spectators, he picked up a fungo bat and promptly drove the ball over the fence and into the stands.

World Championship Results

Rochester, New York winning the men's championship and the Phoenix Ramblers winning the women's championship. The Kodak team became the first team in ASA history to win the men's title twice after winning in 1935. The Ramblers finally won their championship after losing in the semi-finals for three straight years.

The Kodak team had a remarkable record of six consecutive shutouts which began with a 16-0 win over New Hampshire then eliminated District of Columbia 1-0, followed by wins over Connecticut 2-0, Toledo, Ohio 2-0, Buffalo 3-0 and South Bend, Indiana in the championship game 1-0. A majority of newsmen at the tournament agreed that the Rochester Kodak team is one of the best softball teams they have ever seen. Their outstanding pitcher, Harold "Shifty" Gears, pitched some outstanding games, but also was helped by great defensive plays.

The Ramblers women's team stopped Lansing, Michigan, 2-0 winning their way to the semi-finals with an 8-2 win over South Bend, Indiana and a 2-0 win over Oklahoma. With more confidence than prior years, they shutout St. Paul, Minnesota 4-0 in the semi-finals before routing Cleveland 10-3 in the championship game.

A new tournament record was set for the longest game, as Toronto, Canada beat Phoenix 1-0 in 24 innings. Pitcher Cam Ecclestone of Toronto outlasted 17 year old Len Murray from Phoenix, who gave up only nine hits while his teammates got fourteen hits off Ecclestone. The tournament almost made it without rain, but on the final night, a downpour forced the final games to be played on September 10.

The ASA annual meeting was held in Detroit during the tournament and Wilber E. Landis was elected president as was M. J. Pauley secretary. Leo Fischer was elected chairman of the board and B. E. Martin, Newark, New Jersey, Ray Johnson, Nashville, Tennessee and Walter Hakanson, Denver were elected vice presidents. A new gold plated membership pin, measuring just over a half inch, was introduced. It bears a likeness of the ASA emblem with a ball for the background and a diamond over the ball. It will be sold for 35 cents or three for a dollar.

To show appreciation for the effort Landis did for his home town and the tournament, the city of Detroit was awarded the 1941 World's Championship Tournament. It was noted that if not for Raymond Johnson, the ASA could have easily folded. He was known as "crusty on the outside but soft on the inside" by his press box friends. Buck Johnson, former sports editor for the "Chattanooga Times" added, "if there was an angel for the ASA, it was Raymond Johnson."

Michigan Softball Association

Seth Whitmore wrote in the January 1940 issue of "Softball" that "The effort of a few to discredit the ASA failed. At the National AAU Convention, the executive board of that body voted unanimously to continue the alliance with the ASA and lauded our association for its record."

At the annual banquet of the Michigan Softball Association on March 9, 1940, L. H. Weir, director of park recreation planning for the National Recreation Association, described softball as a "major factor tending toward continuance of American democracy."

Weir added, "Softball parks are cheaper to build and maintain and will build stronger character than penal institutions. The next major development in softball would be in the wide-open spaces or rural areas. The federal electrification program has brought electric power to all parts of the nation, and today we find lighted softball playing fields springing up in farming centers."

He pointed out how the development of recreation centers in Cincinnati ended delinquency and stopped a wave of crime among boys in numerous neighborhoods. Weir predicted a thirty-hour work week would become a reality as increased recreational facilities were built. History has shown that this prediction never materialized, but softball certainly filled the void for leisure-time activities.

As the softball season progressed during the summer over twenty new softball facilities had been added across that state with most of the lighted. Ninety-three were sanctioned by the MSA and through their cooperation the organization has grown to its present position of leadership among amateur sport groups in the nation. All parks in which members play must be sanctioned and these parks pay a five percent of their gross gate or collection at inter-city and tournament games to the state association. This accounted for half of the association's income last year.

The regional championship tournament for the upper peninsula was held in Escanaba and was one of the most successful amateur events held in that city in many years. Champions were crowned in four classes and for the first time the upper peninsula will have women in the annual Michigan championships. Winners in each class were: Men's A – Escanaba Paper Mill; B – Nordstrom Motors, Escanaba; C – Traunik; Women's C – Jay Sees, Escanaba.

Michigan's seventh annual state softball tournament was set to open in Lansing on the night of August 30 and continuing until September 3. Champions from district tournaments that were played in 35 cities will compete. Double elimination playoffs will be instituted for the first time for the 54 teams entered out of the

1,000 teams that participated in the district tournaments. Once again Ranney Park along with West Side field and Elm Street park will be used. Practically every city and town in the state is affiliated with the MSA except for Wayne County which has its own organization under the ASA.

Teams from Flint and Niles won four of the eight championship played in Lansing over the Labor Day weekend. Niles won both class C championships, with the Elks winning the men's division and Mutual Drug taking the women's title. Flint won two state trophies with the Yellow Dogs, a negro team winning the men's class A title and Beecher capturing the honor in women's Class B.

The negro team of Pontiac Big Six won the major championship for the second straight year. The women's major was won by VanDervoort's of Lansing for the fourth consecutive year. Mattish Slaughter House of Royal Oak won the men's B title while Daniel's of Saginaw won the tough class A championship.

Two rival associations were being formed in Saginaw by Joe James and Rudy Schmeling, breaking away from the MSA and the ASA. Schmeling is a current member of the MSA state executive board. Both James and Schmeling started out together in organizing the "outlaw" association but they couldn't agree, so each is going their separate ways. James is forming a Saginaw federation while Schmeling is trying to organize a Saginaw Valley Association. An organizational meeting on September drew nine team managers.

It is believed that Michigan now has more lighted softball parks than any other state. Michigan has an excess of 130 lighted fields with scores more expected in 1941.

Seth Whitmore wrote in his article, "Softball Servings" that he hoped for another great year in 1941 instead of being regimented in a march of war. "It pays to play" is a slogan of sporting good dealers, and is well for each of us to have it as a slogan in our daily life too. These are troubling times the world over and unless we relax and continue the sports that have made America great we too may go the way of other democracies, down the path to war and fascism.

He finalized by saying, "It is unfortunate indeed that international conditions have halted the game's growth in other lands. What we say of our game can be said of all American sports. It is truly American and democratic. It is played by people of all nationalities, races, creeds and beliefs. The game teaches tolerance and citizenship. If the boys and girls of Europe could play together as we do in America it would be impossible for dictators to pit them against each other in a war of total destruction." This article shows the importance of how World War II was affecting everyone.

Unfortunately the Japanese attack at Pearl Harbor next year would change everything in America and the world.

CHAPTER FIVE

AMERICA ENTERS WWII, ASA & MSA AFFECTED

WWII Timeline 1941

- January 3 – RAF bombers attack Bremen and the Kiel canal in Germany with the bridge over the canal destroyed.

- January 10 – Lend-Lease agreement introduced into Congress. Germany now controls the air over the Mediterranean Sea. Malta is under attack.

- January 16 – British forces start the first attack on Eastern Africa, with a counter-offensive from Kenya on Italian forces holding Ethiopia.

- January 21 – Tobruk is finally completely taken by British and Australian troops. Romanian Fascists are reportedly executing Jews in Bucharest.

- January 23 – Charles Lindbergh testifies before congress and recommends that the United States negotiates a neutrality pact with Adolf Hitler.

- February 1 – Admiral Husband Kimmel is appointed the Commander of the US Navy in the Pacific.

- February 10 – Malta remains under heavy attack and will be through March.

- February 14 - General Rommel and his Panzer division arrives in Tripoli and the "Afrika Korps" moves eastward towards the British positions.

- March 1 – Hitler gives orders for the expansion of Auschwitz prison camp, to be run by Commandant Rudolf Hoss. Bulgaria signs the Tripartite Pact.

- March 13 – The Luftwaffe which has been bombing the British Isles for weeks, uses heavy forces at Glasgow to bomb the shipping industry.

- March 27 – Japanese spy, Takeo Yoshikawa, arrives in Honolulu and begins to study the United States fleet at Pearl Harbor.

- March 31 – The Afrika Korps continues the German offensive in North Africa moving quickly eastward towards Egypt.

- April 6 – Forces of Germany, Hungary and Italy initiate the invasion of Greece and Yugoslavia. British forces drive the Italian Army out of Addis Ababa, Ethiopia.

- April 12 – Belgrade, Yugoslavia surrenders. The Germans defeat Commonwealth forces at the Battle of Vevi.

- April 13 – Malta is bombed again as it remains a thorn in the side of German supply movements in the Mediterranean. Japan and the Soviet Union sign a neutrality pact.

- April 21 – About 223,000 Greek soldiers in Albania surrender as their retreat is cut off by the German advance.

- April 23 – The British military and civilians along with the Greek government evacuate to the island of Crete. Churchill is determined to defend it.

- April 27 – Greece surrenders as Athens is occupied by German forces.

- April 30 – After another failure, Rommel is ordered to stop attacking Tobruk.

- May 1 – Liverpool is almost destroyed after seven nights of bombing.

- May 8 – U-boats cause heavy convoy losses in the Atlantic, however U-110 is captured and another "enigma" machine is discovered and saved.

- May 12 – The RAF strike German cities of Berlin, Hamburg and Emden

- May 20 – German paratroopers land on Crete, a seven day battle begins.

- May 21 – The US merchant ship, SS Robin Moor, is sunk by U-69. This startles the nation and President Roosevelt announces an "unlimited national emergency."

- May 25 - British battlecruiser HMS Hood is sunk by the massive battleship, Bismarck in the north Atlantic. The Greek government leaves Crete for Cairo.
- May 27 – The Bismarck is sunk by the Royal Navy after a damaged steering system forced it into an endless series of circular movements.
- June 6 – More British fighter planes are sent to Malta as Luftwaffe attacks continue.
- June 13 – Soviets begin deporting Lithuanians to Siberia prison camps. After five days, 35,000 are sent among them 7,000 Jews.
- June 15 – "Operation Battleaxe" by the British fails to relieve the siege of Tobruk. The British are badly defeated at Halfaya Pass, called "Hell-fire Pass"
- June 16 – All German and Italian consulates in the United States are ordered closes and their staff to leave the country by July 10.
- June 22 – Germany invades the Soviet Union with "Operation Barbarossa". It's a three-pronged attack at Leningrad, Moscow and the oil fields of Caucasus. Romania invades the southern border siding with Germany.
- June 24 – German forces along with Lithuanian militia in Vilnius kill dozens of Jews on the streets, with civilian spectators cheering them on.

- June 25 – The Soviet Union bombs Helsinki, Finland announcing a state of war exists between Finland and the Soviet Union.

- June 26 – Hungary and Slovakia declare war on the Soviet Union. Albania soon follows.

- June 29 – German and Finnish troops begin "Operation Arctic Fox" against the Soviet Union.

- July 1 – All American men over the age of 21 are required to register for the draft.

- July 6 – British torpedo planes sink and Italian destroyer at Tobruk. The Ecuadorian-Peruvian War conflict begins in South America.

- July 8 – Britain and the Soviet Union sign a mutual defense agreement, promising not to sign any form of separate peace agreement with Germany.

- July 10 – Germany occupies Latvia and German troops advance into the Ukraine.

- July 15 – The Red Army starts a counter-attack against the Wehrmacht near Leningrad.

- July 21 – The Luftwaffe launch air strikes on Moscow.

- July 26 – In response to the Japanese occupation of French Indochina, president Roosevelt orders the seizure of all Japanese assets in the U.S.

- July 28 – The Germans solidify their presence in the Baltic states; native Jewish populations of the Baltic states are exterminated.

- July 31 – Under the direction of Hitler, Hermann Goring orders SS general Reinhard Heydrich to submit a "final solution" of the Jewish question.

- August 1 – The U.S. announces an oil embargo against "aggressors". Japan occupies Saigon, Vietnam.

- August 5 – The Weirmarck trap Red Army forces in Smolensk and take 300,000 soldiers prisoners. The city of Orel is taken.

- August 9 – President Roosevelt and Winston Churchill meet in Newfoundland and the Atlantic Charter is created, signed and released to the World press.

- August 11 – After months of attacks, Malta is relieved by a convoy.

- August 12 – Hitler, against the advice of his generals, shifts some forces from the Moscow front to Leningrad and Crimean offensives.

- August 18 – Because of heavy German protests, Hitler orders a temporary halt of systematic euthanasia of the mentally ill and handicapped.

- August 22 – German forces close in on Leningrad as citizens build improvised fortifications.

- September 1 – With the assistance of Finnish armies to the north, Leningrad is officially cut off.

- September 4 – The USS Greer becomes the first military ship fired upon by a German U-boat even though the U.S. is still a neutral power.

- September 6 – Japanese Imperial conference decides Japan will go to war with the U.S. if the oil embargo is not lifted.

- September 8 – As German forces drive further into Leningrad; Stalin orders the Volga Germans deported to Siberia.

- September 19 – Kiev falls to the German troops. The Red Army suffers heavy casualties trying to defend this city in Soviet Ukraine.

- September 26 – The U.S. Naval Command orders an all-out war on Axis shipping in American waters.

- September 28 – German SS troops kill over 30,000 Jews on the outskirts of Kiev.

- October 2 – German forces launch "Operation Typhoon" against Moscow. Soviet hero, general Zhukov, will lead the defense of the capital.

- October 7 – Mass destruction occurs in Berlin, Ruhr, and Cologne because of night time bombing by the RAF.

- October 10 – German armies encircle about 660,000 Red Army troops near Vyasma. Some make a glowing prediction of the end of the war.

- October 14 – Heavy snow and falling temperatures halt the German tanks on the Moscow front.

- October 17 – The first American casualties of the war happens when eleven sailors are killed aboard the USS Kearny which is torpedoed by U-568 near Iceland.

- October 18 – Red Army reinforcements arrive in Moscow from Siberia. General Hideki Tojo is named Japan's 40th prime minister after prime minister Konoye collapses.

- October 22 – After a delayed bomb planted by Soviets killed 67 people at the Romanian headquarters, the "Odessa massacre" begins and continues for two days. About 34,000 Jews are led in a long line and shot and killed in an anti-tank ditch. 35,000 Jews are expelled to the Ghetto and are left in freezing conditions for 10 days. Many die from this.

- October 27 – German forces reach Sevastopol in the Crimea, but the tanks are slowed or immobilized entirely by deep mud.

- October 31 – The destroyer USS Reuben James is torpedoed by U-552 near Iceland, killing more than 100 U.S. Navy sailors.

- November 1 – President Roosevelt announces that the U.S. Coast Guard will now be under the direction of the U.S. Navy.

- November 4 – Hirohito approves the attack on Pearl Harbor.

- November 7 – Another night of bombings by the RAF on Berlin, Ruhr, and Cologne causes heavy losses.

- November 12 – Temperatures around Moscow drop to minus 14 degrees and the Soviets launch ski troops. A squadron of fighters arrives at Malta by the HMS Ark Royal. The ship is struck by torpedoes by U-81 and sinks the next day.

- November 17 – Joseph Grew, the U.S. ambassador to Japan, cables the state department that Japan had plans to launch an attack on Pearl Harbor (this was ignored).

- November 18 – British Commonwealth and other Allied troops launch "Operation Crusader" and cross into Libya and temporarily relieve the siege of Tobruk.

- November 22 – Rommel begins a counteroffensive just south of Tobruk which the allies had taken days earlier. British tanks suffer heavy losses.

- November 24 – Rommel meets no opposition as he moves into Egypt.

- November 26 – A Japanese attack fleet of 33 warships, auxiliary craft, six aircraft carriers, sails from northern Japan for the Hawaiian Islands. The Hull note ultimatum is delivered to Japan by the United States.

- November 27 – Rommel retreats from Egypt to refuel which allows the 8th Army to temporarily relieve the forces in Tobruk

- November 28 – German panzers are on the outskirts of Moscow.

- December 1 – SS officer Karl Jaeger reports Lithuania is "clean of Jews".

- December 3 – The United Kingdom announces that all men between 18 and 50 years of age will have to serve. Women will serve in fire brigades and in auxiliary groups.

- December 4 – The temperature on the Moscow front falls to minus 31 degrees Fahrenheit. German attacks are failing.

- December 5 – Germans call off the attack on Moscow, just 11 miles away. The Red Army counter-attacks during a heavy blizzard.

- December 7 – The Japanese Imperial Navy launches a sneak attack on Pearl Harbor. Battle ship row is suffering huge casualties. It coincides with attacks on Thailand, Guam, Hong Kong, the Philippines, Shanghai, Singapore and

Wake Island.

- December 8 – The United States, United Kingdom, Netherlands, and New Zealand declare war on Japan.

- December 10 – British battlecruiser HMS Repulse and battleship HMS Prince of Wales are sunk in a Japanese air attack in the South China Sea.

- December 11 – Germany and Italy declare war on the United States. The United States reciprocates by declaring war on Germany and Italy.

- December 13 – Islands around the Philippines are taken by Japan under general Homma.

- December 14 – After the British cruiser HMS Galatea is sunk by U-557 off Alexandria, the allies suffer numerous naval defeats.

- December 16 – Commonwealth troops push Rommel back and he orders a withdrawal all the way to El Agheila, where he began in March.

- December 19 – Hitler becomes Supreme Commander-in-chief of the German Army.

- December 20 – The battle for Wake Island continues with several Japanese ships sunk or damaged. Stanislawow ghetto completely closed from the outside and sealed with walls.

- December 21 – The siege of Leningrad continues and an

estimated 3,000 citizens are dying each day from starvation and various diseases.

- December 22 – The Japanese land on the northern port of Luzon in the Philippines.
- December 23 – A second Japanese landing on Wake Island is successful, and the American garrison surrenders after hours of fighting.
- December 24 – American forces retreat unto the Bataan Peninsula in the Philippines.
- December 27 – British and Norwegian commandos raid the Norwegian port of Vagsoy, forcing Hitler to reinforce the garrison and defenses.

How the ASA is affected by WWII

1941

Although the United States didn't officially get involved in WWIII until December 8, 1941, the ASA was affected during the year in regards to the need for men and women for the war effort.

As more and more men and women entered the work force needed in factories to build and supply equipment to those countries who signed the Lend Lease Agreement, recreational sports were affected as well as professional sports. industrial leagues formed throughout the country which filled a need, but team registrations began to take a dip late in the year.

Leo Fischer, past president and now chairman of the board, resigned over what he though was commercialism taking over the sport. Fischer wrote in a letter to ASA President Wilber E. Landis, dated April 18, 1941, "I would like to go on record at the spring meeting against the proposed tie-up with Pepsi-Cola or any organization sponsoring a commercial product for our world's championship tournament. Regardless of the need for financial aid, it would be a very serious back step for the organization." He added, "I felt it was a big advance when you induced us to move the tournament to Detroit with the promise of civic backing, even though this newspaper (Chicago American) never asked anything from the ASA except goodwill."

"The world's championship meet is the top event of our entire program. It is as inconceivable as it would be to have Coca-Cola sponsor the baseball World Series or Royal Crown the Olympic Games. I like to drink Pepsi-Cola and that company is to be commended for its interest in softball and other amateur sports, but you can be certain that underwriting the world's championship is not being done from a purely altruistic standpoint. Their advertising men are put in the same class with other promotion, such as sky-writing, magazine ads, etc., used to aid the sale of Pepsi-Cola." Fischer finished the letter by saying, "I, for one, feel that the highest honor in amateur softball should not be made on the basis of a sale promotion for a soft drink, nor any commercial product, regardless of its merits."

The ASA's ties with soft-drink companies began in 1941 when

Pepsi-Cola initially sponsored the World's Softball championships. The agreement was announced at the spring meeting of ASA on April 19, 1941. Secretary Pauley said that the "Pepsi-Cola Company was to give each state or metro association, in good standing, a 30 inch trophy with a $50 retail value, to their men's champion."

"The same would be given to each state or metro girl's champ whose entry fee into the World's Championship had been paid by the national treasury. The world championship trophies, team and individual, are also to be given by the Pepsi-Cola Company."

Sportsman Park of Ann Arbor, Michigan filed an official protest with ASA president W. E. Landis after the People's Credit Jewelry team in Toronto, Canada for failure to show up for an event to benefit the British war effort. All receipts were to go to war relief and this event was arranged and advertised with considerable expense.

The letter requested that People's Credit Jewelry be suspended for the rest of the season. The protest read as follows: "Sportsman Park of Ann Arbor through the person of Walter F. Frey, hereby, enters a complaint against the People's Credit Jewelry softball team of Toronto, Ontario for failing to make an appearance for a scheduled game on Sunday, August 10, 1941. The protest was filed but no action was taken by ASA officials.

A letter from Walter S. Mack, president of Pepsi-Cola was read to the delegates at the annual meeting. "Indeed a pleasure for the

Pepsi-Cola Company to be associated with the ASA as sponsor of the 1941 World Amateur Softball Championships. We are fully aware of the esteemed reputation your association now enjoys and we are confident that this tournament will uphold the standards of clean sportsmanship and hard competition that had prevailed in the past."

The ninth World's Softball Championship Tournament will once again take place in Detroit beginning September 10 and finishing up on September 14. Teams from almost all states will compete along with several teams from Canada and one from Puerto Rico. It is estimated that a record 108 teams will compete this year. Games will take place Belle Isle, Northwestern field, and under the lights at Mack Park in Dearborn, Eloise and the Michigan Alkali field in Wyandotte. Semi-finals and finals will take place at the U. of D. stadium Saturday and Sunday respectfully.

Wednesday evening there will be a parade of teams at the University of Detroit stadium followed by two games by the Kodak Park of Rochester, New York, last year's defending champs and defending women's champions, the Ramblers from Phoenix, Arizona. They will receive an automatic berth due to winning last year. The teams competing against them will be drawn from a hat by Michigan governor Murray D. VanWagoner.

The Ramblers are led by Amelina Peralta, the ace pitcher of the team and a .410 batting average, and Marjorie Wood, who had a season average of .450. Helping Peralta on the mound will be Louise Curtis, who in 1937, won three in one day in this tournament and Charlotte Armstrong. Dot Wilkinson, rated one of the best players in the game, has a .446 average and just turned eighteen years old. She was a member of the team in 1933, which is truly remarkable. Fan favorite, Harold "shifty" Gears will once again be on the mound for the Kodak team. His famous figure-eight windup has drawn packed crowds just to see him pitch.

Another fan favorite team, the all negro Big Six team from Pontiac, Michigan will be without their star player, second baseman, Ruby Taylor, who was drafted into the service of his country. Taylor has been with the team since he was just thirteen years old.

Results of the men's major tournament: In the semi-finals, Ed Kizelevich, of Phelps Dodge from Elizabeth, New Jersey tosses a no-hitter but lost a tough 1-0 game against the Romancos (Rosemary's Manufacturing Company) from Roanoke Rapids, North Carolina. The other semi-final game saw Bendix Brakes, South Bend, Indiana beating the Briggs team from Detroit, 7-2 behind Stan Corgan's pitching and Vince Piotrowski's three hits.

Corgan came on in the last inning In relief of Big Ike Bierwagen in the championship game to preserve a 9 -0 shutout over Romancos. Russ DuBarry of Romancos went 5-1, pitching four shutouts until the finals, when he was forced to leave the game when the Bendix team jumped all over him. They kept hitting the ball and finished with fourteen hits. Bendix finished the season with 38 straight wins.

MVP – Ike "Bonecrusher" Bierwagen with a 3-0 record, pitched a scoreless eight innings in the championship game and contributed a double.

Outstanding Pitcher – Russ DuBarry with a 5-1 record, four shutouts, and pitched 61 consecutive innings.

The only results found regarding the girls worls's championship tournament was the Higgins Midgets team of Tulsa, Oklahoma winning by beating the Jax team from New Orleans, 1-0, Led by pitcher, Nina Korgan, who struck out seventeen batters. During one game, Korgan fanned 20 of the 21 batters she faced in a perfect game. During the war she would compete against various armed forces men's teams.

Nina Korgan was named unofficial MVP and Outstanding Pitcher. Olympia Savona was the batting leader; .412 average, 6 runs, 4 RBI's and two home runs.

In 1941, the ASA had more than 300,000 players competing and more than one hundred million fans, according to president Landis.

How the war affected MSA in 1941

Harry Harrell is named head of the state association protest board. He was one of the best known players in the state before retiring and taking on the roll of Organizing leagues and umpiring a few years ago. He will also be one of the umpires in the state tournament this year.

State Commissioner, Seth Whitmore reported that this season has been disappointing in some areas where fighting between teams, players, and managers has become intolerable. Rules haven't been in writing, no record of contracts have been kept, and other rules have been violated. This problem has caused a lack of fan interest.

He stated that many lessons can be learned from this, the most important being no local community should depend on one individual that the league folds because he quits or leaves town. Parks and leagues should be organized that they will continue on regardless of leadership. The MSA has a great set of rules and regulations and when followed there seems to be no trouble. However, MSA has no jurisdiction over local leagues and that is where the trouble lies.

Midland can now boast that they have one of the finest pitchers in the game, Clyde Dexter, of the Chemical City Athletic team. With an excellent fast ball, he moved to Midland from Toledo, Ohio and made a quick name for himself. During the season he tossed several no-hitters and had shutouts against the famed Kodak team from Rochester, New York. He also shutout the big bats of Briggs from Detroit.

One of the veteran opposing players exclaimed, "I thought Justice was fast (referring to Charles Justice of the Big Six team), but that boy Dexter really burns them in."

The new rules under which girls teams played this season have been widely debated. This year, for the first time, men coaches were prohibited from coaching on the field and girls had to learn to coach at first and third base. Also, girls under the age of 16 were not allowed to play unless they had their sixteenth birthday by January 1, 1942. The girls are also prohibited from playing more than three games in one week.

Some feel the new rules have hurt the game while others claim they have helped. Next spring, this should be a hot topic when the MSA has their annual meeting.

There will be new rules instituted for the Michigan softball state tournament this year.

1. Teams must have 10 players at the start and throughout the game.
2. All teams must be on the field ready to play at the scheduled time or they will forfeit.
3. Once the lineup has been turned in to the scorer, no changes can be made
4. There shall be no smoking or profane language used on the playing field or in the dugouts.
5. Teams will be allowed to add up to two extra players from their own region. These teams must select players from their own class of play or lower.
6. Girls must provide absolute proof of age. Accepted proof is birth certificate, driver's license, school affidavit or notarized statement.

7. Major teams must follow the rule regarding pitcher's uniform. Other classes may wear any uniform not confusing to the batter, except white or light gray.

The eighth annual Michigan Softball Association state tournament will again be played in Lansing. Fifty-two teams from the nine regions will begin play on Friday night, August 29 and continue through Labor Day weekend with Tuesday, September 2 being the night of the finals.

The Majors and Class A will play a double elimination format while the other classes will play a single elimination and decide champions on Monday, September 1. Ranney Park will continue to host the finals while the other three municipal fields will play all day and night during the weekend.

The Big Six team will return to defend their major title in hopes of a third straight, while the VanDervoort's girls team from Lansing will seek their fifth straight title in the major division. Michigan is the only state that conducts state tournaments for more than two classes.

As expected, favorites; Big Six, Pontiac and VanDervoorts, Lansing won their third and fifth straight state titles respectively. Other winners were: Men's Class A, Old Milwaukee, Muskegon; Class B, Elks, Niles; and Class C, 1900 Corp., St Joseph. Women's Class A, Roverettes, Grand Rapids; Class B, Sutton Sales, Saginaw; Class C, Champayne, Muskegon. The Big Six team and VanDervoorts team will now play in the ASA world's championship tournament in Detroit.

A few years ago the Autos of St. Joseph established a great record when they won the Michigan major softball championship for three consecutive years. They had one of the best teams in the country and it was believed their record would stand for years to come. It didn't last long as the Big Six team from Pontiac matched their record last year as they won their third straight title.

The all negro ten actually has a greater record than the Autos, as they previously won the world's negro championship and also won the Tri-state title in 1939.

In the September, 1941 issue of Softball, Seth Whitmore wrote, "While the world is torn with strife, bloodshed, race hatred and intolerance, here in America we live and play together, enjoying a democracy that is constantly improving despite the great concentration of power in Washington. Gathered at this year's world championships here in Detroit, we have players of all races, creeds and nationalities. Rich and poor, young and old they play together in the great game that plays such an important part in our American way of life."

Whitmore finished by saying, "On the softball diamond we find the C.I.O. matched against the Chamber of Commerce, the Knights of Columbus against the DeMolay and so on down the line. They play with but one thought in mind, the game and the fun of winning."

1942

Timeline of World War II

- January 2 – Manila is captured by the Japanese forces. American and Filipino forces continue retreating into Bataan.

- January 7 – Operation Barbarossa is failing as the Red Army pushes back the German forces about 155 miles from Moscow. The siege of Bataan begins.

- January 11 – Japanese troops capture Kuala Lumpur, Malaya.

- January 20 – The Nazis decide that the final solution to the Jewish problem is relocation and later extermination.

- January 24 – American troops land in Samoa in an effort to stop the Japanese into the Pacific.

- January 26 – The first American troops land in Europe in Northern Ireland.

- January 29 – Rommel's Afrika Korps recaptures Benghazi, Libya.

- February 1 – The U.S. automobile industry stop production of cars and switches over to defense building.

- February 11 – The U.S. carrier, Saratoga is torpedoed by the Japanese sub I-6 about 480 miles north of Pearl Harbor.

- February 15 – Singapore falls to the Japanese forces. One of the worst defeats in British military history.

- February 19 – Japanese aircraft attack Darwin in Australia's Northern Territory.

- February 22 – President Roosevelt order general MacArthur to evacuate the Philippines as American defense collapses.

- February 25 – The internment of Japanese-American citizens in the Western United States begins.

- February 28 – The Japanese land forces invade Java.

- March 3 – A surprise raid by Japanese aircraft on the airfield and harbor of Broome, Western Australia.

- March 6 – Malta receives more fighter aircraft for its ongoing defense.

- March 9 – Japanese forces enter Rangoon, Burma and now control Burma, Java and New Guinea. They have plans to invade Australia next.

- March 12 – American troops land in New Caledonia with its next target to use as a staging base for the eventual invasion of Guadacanal.

- March 14 – Japanese land troops in the Solomon Islands and want to use Guadalcanal also as air bases against Australia. American forces are being trapped in Manila Bay and the retreat to Corregidor begins.

- March 22 – A fractured convoy reaches Malta after the Luftwaffe and Italian sea forces suffer heavy losses.

- March 28 – British commandos launch Operation Chariot, a raid on the port of Saint Nazaire, France. The HMS Campbelltown is filled with explosives and using a time-delay fuse, rams the dock gates, explodes, and the port is completely destroyed and unable to resume service until 1947.

- April 2 – Over 24,000 severely sick and starving American and Filipino troops are now trapped on the Bataan Peninsula.

- April 4 – Hitler issues Directive 41, outlining his plans for the summer offensive in Russia. Main objective to seize much needed oil fields.

- April 9 – Japanese Navy launches air raids on Ceylon. Royal Navy carrier, HMS Hermes and Royal Australian destroyer HMAS Vampire are sunk. The Bataan death march begins as prisoners are marched to detention camps.

- April 18 – The famous general Doolittle raid on Nagoya, Japan begins as B-25s take off from the USS Hornet. The raid is a great boost for morale.

- April 20 – Churchill decides to replace general Dobbie of Malta with Lord Gort. The USS Wasp delivers 47 Spitfire

Mk V fighters to Malta but the planes are destroyed mostly on the ground by intense Axis air raids.

- April 23 – Luftwaffe raids on English towns such as Exeter, Bath, Norwich and York begins and will last into early June.

- May 6 – General Jonathon Wainwright surrenders the last U.S. forces in the Philippines to Lt. general Homma. About 12,000 troops are made prisoners.

- May 7 – After several naval battles in the Coral Sea, by sure luck, the light carrier is sited and sunk by planes from the USS Lexington and USS Yorktown.

- May 8 – the Japanese and American Navies located each other's carriers and the air battle begins. The Japanese carrier Zuikaku escapes but the Shokaku has its flight deck severely bent. The Lexington is sunk and Yorktown damaged.

- May 9 – The USS Wasp and HMS Eagle deliver a second squadron of Spitfires to Malta. These aircraft used more effectively than the previous ones, turn the tide in the skies over Malta and the Axis is forced to abandon daylight bombing.

- May 12 – German sub U-553 sinks British freighter Nicoya near the mouth of the St. Lawrence Seaway.

- May 23 – German tanks meet up at Balakleya, southwest of Kharkov, encircling most of the Soviets' sixth and ninth

Armies.

- May 27 – British use American Sherman tanks in an effort to stop Rommel's attacks on the Gazala line. The Rommel offensive will last well into June.

- May 31 – Japanese midget subs sink a support ship in Sydney harbor. The use of spitfires over Malta is proving to be a success. Rommel's offensive has stalled well short of Tobruk, due to resistance by the British first and seventh armored division.

- June 1 – Reports are coming in that gas is being used on Jews at concentration camps to the East.

- June 3 – Japan launches air raids against Alaska in the Aleutian Islands. The Japanese fleet, with four carriers, under Admiral Nagumo decides to attack Midway's land-based air defenses after failing to find any U.S. carriers.

- June 4 – The great sea battle at Midway begins when carriers, USS Hornet, Yorktown and Lexington dive bombers find the flight decks of carriers, Akagi, Kaga, and Soryu crowded with fuel lines and explosive ordnances. They are soon fully engulfed in flames with only the Hiryu able to escape. The Japanese find the Yorktown, it is badly damaged and abandoned. The next day the Hiryu is sunk after giving its position away to hit the Yorktown.

- June 7 – Japanese invade Attu and Kiska, the first invasion of American soil in 128 years. The battle of Midway ends with the Yorktown sinking and all four Japanese carriers and a cruiser sunk. The battle is the turning point in the war.

- June 13 – Rommel does great damage to the British armor. The 50th and 1st South African division are threatened with complete encirclement.

- June 15 – After Churchill asks general Auchinleck what the status is at Tobruk, he replies, "We have no intention whatever of giving up Tobruk."

- June 16   Operation Vigorous and Harpoon convoys sent to supply Malta are heavily damaged and only two ships arrive at the port.

- June 17 – Tobruk is now completely surrounded.

- June 18 – The beginning of the approach to use nuclear bombs begins when the "Manhattan Project" begins.

- June 21 – Tobruk falls and 35,000 men are captured. Rommel's tanks are assisted by Luftwaffe attacks. The road to Egypt in now open.

- June 24 – General Dwight D. Eisenhower arrives in London to be Commander of American forces in Europe.

- July 3 - The battle of El Alamein begins as Rommel attacks British forces. Within four days they are stalemated as he lacks enough ammunition.

- July 16 – On orders from the Vichy French government headed by Pierre Laval, French police arrest 13,152 Jews, they will be sent to Auschwitz.

- July 22 – The systematic deportation of Jews from the Warsaw Ghetto begins. Treblinka II, an extermination camp is opened in Poland.

- July 24 – The Red Army is in retreat along the Don River.

- July 27 – The RAF uses massive incendiary bombs on Hamburg.

- August 3 – A convoy to Malta is decimated by the Luftwaffe and U-boats.

- August 7 – "Operation Watchtower" begins the Guadalcanal campaign as American forces invade Gavutu, Guadalcanal, Tulagi and Tanambogo.

- August 10 – Rommel begins another attack around El Alamein, but by September he is back to his original lines.

- August 11 – The HMS Eagle, a carrier on route to Malta, is torpedoed and sinks with heavy loss of life. Four merchant ships and a tanker from the convoy get through.

- August 17 – The first U.S. Army Air Forces B-17 heavy

bombers raid in France targets railroad yards in Rouen, France.

- August 19 – "Operation Jubilee", a raid by British and Canadian forces on Dieppe, France is a disaster. Most are killed or captured by German defenders.

- August 20 – Henderson air field on Guadalcanal receives its first American fighter planes.

- August 21 – Hundreds of Japanese troops are killed at Henderson air field after a failed banzai charge.

- August 23 – A massive German air raid on Stalingrad.

- August 27 – Marshall Georgii Zhukov is appointed commander of Stalingrad defenses.

- August 28 – Incendiary bombs dropped by a Japanese seaplane causes a forest fire in Oregon.

- September 3 – Battle of Stalingrad is officially underway. The Red Army has to use civilian men and boys to help stave off the German forces.

- September 5 – The Japanese suffer their first defeat when American and Australian forces force them off the Island of Papua.

- September 13 – Stalingrad is completely surrounded by German forces.

- September 15 – The carrier, USS Wasp is sunk by a Japanese sub off the coast of Guadalcanal.

- September 20 – The RAF bombs Munich, Duesseldorf and Saarbrucken.

- September 23 – Japanese naval bombardment and landing forces nearly destroy Henderson field on Guadalcanal. After four days they're beaten back.

- September 28 – The Japanese continue their retreat back down the Kokoda Track in New Guinea. This will ease the tensions of an attack on Australia.

- October 3 – The first successful launch of the A4-rocket in Germany. It will be the first man-made object reaching space with a height of 84.5 kilometers.

- October 7 – The U.S. Navy intercept and defeat a Japanese fleet on the way to Guadalcanal for reinforcements. A cruiser and several destroyers are sunk.

- October 12 – The Red Army method of ferrying troops across the Volga, into Stalingrad seems to be success, as the German advance comes to a halt.

- October 18 – Hitler orders all captured commandos to be executed. Admiral William "Bull" Halsey is given command of the South Pacific naval forces.

- October 24 – U.S. naval task force 34, departs Hampton Roads, Virginia: "Operation Torch" begins with general

Patton destined for North Africa.

- October 26 – The naval battle of Santa Cruz results in Japanese losing many aircraft and two carriers heavily damaged. However, the USS Enterprise is damaged and the carrier USS Hornet is sunk.

- October 31 – The British breakthrough at El Alamein with tanks. Rommel's mine fields fail to stop the allied armor.

- November 3 – The second battle of El Alamein ends with Rommel's German forces retreating during the night.

- November 8 – "Operation Torch" begins with the allied invasion of Morocco and Algeria. The U.S. 1ˢᵗ Armored Division lands east and west of Oran.

- November 10   Montgomery begins a major British offensive and reach Bardia, Tobruk, and Benghazi in three days. Montgomery is knighted and made a full general. Churchill speaks, "This is not the end. It is not even the beginning of the end. But it is, perhaps, the end of the beginning."

- November 11 – Convoys reach Malta. The island is relieved of its siege.

- November 12 – A climatic naval battle near Guadalcanal begins between Japanese and American forces. The Red Army attempts to relieve Stalingrad.

- November 13 – The battle for Guadalcanal has aviators sinking the battleship Hiei. The USS Juneau is sunk with most of the crew including the five Sullivan brothers.

- November 15 – The battle for Guadalcanal ends. Although the U.S. Navy suffers heavy losses, it maintains control of the water around the island.

- November 18 – The RAF has few losses as the bombers strike Berlin.

- November 19 – General Zhukov launches "Operation Uranus" to try and encircle the German army in the city of Stalingrad.

- November 22 – General Paulus sends a telegram to Hitler saying that the German 6th Army is trapped and surrounded in Stalingrad.

- November 23 – Hitler orders general Paulus to hold at all cost.

- December 1 – Gasoline rationing begins in America. The U.S. cruiser Northampton is sunk by Japanese destroyers as they attempt to come down "the slot' to Guadalcanal.

- December 2 – The first nuclear chain reaction is initiated at the University of Chicago. A coded message, "The Italian navigator has landed in the New World" is sent to president Roosevelt.

- December 9 – The marines turn over Guadalcanal to the American army.
- December 12 – Rommel retreats to Tripoli. The Germans attempt to rescue its forces trapped in Stalingrad with "Operation Winter Storm."
- December 15 – American and Australian troops finally push Japanese troops out of Buna, New Guinea.
- December 26 – Heavy fighting continues on Guadalcanal on Mount Austen in the west.
- December 31 – The year is ending on a brighter note: Rommel is trapped in Tunisia, The Germans are encircled at Stalingrad and the Japanese appear ready to abandon Guadalcanal.

The ASA in 1942

The war is beginning to take a toll on the playing of softball in America. Men were being drafted by the thousands each month to serve in the armed forces. Women were needed to work in the factories to take their place and help build equipment, guns, ammunition, tanks, and bombers.

There was an increase in industrial leagues but the hours of work was making it difficult to play softball and maintain the household. Lighted fields were reduced for play because of the need for keeping America "dark". The shortage of civilian teams was offset by the growth of defense plant clubs and 67,000 service teams.

Softball grew in the European and Pacific theatres as men began to play softball to ease tensions and they were encouraged by their superiors to play to stay healthy. In fact softball equipment was being sent to aid in this effort. Servicemen helped to popularize the game. Before long, teams were formed from every company, be they officers, NCO's, enlisted men, wing commands, motor pools, etc.

The 1942 World Championship tournament would limit the women's division to just 10 teams because of travel restrictions. With the reduction, a double elimination format was implemented which would prove to be so popular it would stay for the following tournaments.

The United States was divided into fifteen regions and were to hold regional tournaments to keep travel to a member. By reducing the number of teams, in the national tournament to be held in Detroit, the ASA was able to hold a double elimination format which became popular for the men as well. Some teams from the northwestern part of the U.S. didn't participate in the past because travel expenses didn't justify playing just one game and being sent home.

Pepsi-Cola didn't renew its option to sponsor the awards for the 1942 World's Championship tournament because of a lack of cooperation by the state and metro commissioners, according to secretary Pauley. That year, Pauley also used ASA funds to pay off more than $7,000 in debts, some back to 1938, leaving nothing in the bank account. Except for the back salary ($8,860) owed to Pauley, the ASA wasn't indebted to any individual or firm.

Due to the fact of Pepsi-Cola pulling out its sponsorship, Coca-Cola was contacted and ASA president Johnson would later write, "The Coca-Cola people were wonderful to us from the first time I mentioned the possibility of Coca-Cola sponsoring softball to the late Bill Kaliska in December of 1942.

When the national championships wrapped up in Detroit, the men's major champions were the Deep Rock Oilers from Tulsa, Oklahoma. They defeated the very strong Briggs Beautyware Bombers, of Detroit 2-0 on a one-hitter in the title game, behind the pitching of Sig Lawson. During the regionals, Lawson and Al Linde tossed three perfect games, and the lanky six foot, three inch Lawson pitched four games in the nationals, a total of 36 innings, while allowing only two runs, both unearned.

The Jax Maids from New Orleans, won the women's division after losing to the Garden City Maids of Chicago in the championship game forcing a second game to be played as the Jax Maids suffered their first loss. Nina Korgan, who pitched for the Higgins Midgets the year before, had her shutout string broke at 57.2 scoreless innings, after her 1-0 win against the Arizona Ramblers.

Korgan went into the 7th inning of the championship game with a 1-0 lead before Garden City Maids after two were out, pushed across four runs to win 4 –1. Lottie Jackson started the final game for the Jax Maids and she was supported by four runs in the first inning with a bunt single, an errant throw on another bunt, a base hit, then base hits by Jackson and Dottie Pitts scored three runs. Nina Korgan came in and pitched the last three innings to preserve the win. Sonny Berger and Shirley Dressander were the pitchers of record for the Garden City Maids. Korgan was the unofficial MVP and Jo Leonard, Garden City Maids was the batting leader with a .500 average.

Michigan Softball Association

Michigan was no different than the rest of the country when the second year of WWII was in progress. Like the ASA, the MSA saw many leagues affected in the amount of players involved in playing softball. So many men were being drafted which was the largest reason and women entering the work force and having to care for children at home was the other reason for the decrease in players.

Once players diminished in large numbers and fan favorites were no longer playing, then leagues began to decrease in numbers. Of Fans stopped attending games so the need to build more fields and light them was no longer needed. State commissioner Seth Whitmore didn't realize how much of an effect WWII would have on the game of softball, or for that matter, all sports in America.

Early in the year, Seth Whitmore wrote in "Softball" newsletter: "Softball has attained it present condition as America's No. 1

pastime for many reasons. It is not our purpose to go into the history of the game, but in passing it is well to mention a few of the things that have made softball great, and to urge those who love the sport to see that nothing ever happens that will cause the interest to decline."

"First we might emphasize that softball is popular because it is a game for all. This is of great importance in this day and age when we are devoting so much of our time to the use of leisure. In softball we have a game for the young and old, The girls and women as well as their brothers and husbands, and a game that draws no class lines due to race, creed, religion, or financial position."

"Secondly, softball is popular because it is a game that can be played without excessive cost. Under municipal recreation programs, in the industrial plants, and within the confines of private parks the best games are played with a low admission fee or without charge at all. This makes it possible for the masses to enjoy a wholesome outdoor sport that is not above their means."

"Softball is great because it is an amateur sport. Only in very rare cases it has been possible for professional promotors to exploit players for personal gain, and in these cases it has not lasted long. It must be stressed that, when attempts are made to commercialize softball, the game declines and interest is lost. It must remain, first, last and always an amateur recreation."

"The game is clean. Softball is played with a minimum of disputes because it attracts those who play for fun. It is also well organized under the banner of the Amateur Softball Association and its affiliated bodies which impose severe penalties for unsportsmanlike conduct and other acts that hurt the game."

Metro Detroit would welcome the long awaited clash between the Briggs Bombers, defending Class A men's softball champions, and Fruehauf will take place on Sunday night reports the "Detroit Evening Times" on August 16, 1942. Briggs also played in the World's Championship tournament in Detroit last year.

The Detroit Naval Recreational Fund, created to provide entertainment facilities for sailors stationed in Detroit, was enriched by $27,000 with the purchase of 25,000 tickets to the World Championship tournament semi-finals to be played in Detroit. The Teamsters International Council 43 made the offer to the ASA to put the fund over the top was culminated by Thornton Brodhead, administrator of the recreational fund, with the presentation of the huge check by Barbara Hoffa, daughter of Jimmy Hoffa. With this purchase the semi-finals to be held at U. of Detroit will most assuredly be a sellout. All proceeds from the tournament goes to the Navy fund.

The MSA state championships were played in Lansing and the following women's teams won their respective divisions: Major – Dad's Root Beer, Ann Arbor; Class A – Shippee Fisher, Owosso; Class B – Saginaw Transfer, Saginaw; Class C – Flashes, Saginaw. The men's state champions were: Major – Dow A.C., Midland; Class A – Wilcox Rich, Saginaw; Class B – Earl Coal, Ferndale;

and Class C – Stubnitz-Green, Adrian. Dow A.C. and Dad's Root Beer would represent MSA in the National Championship tournament in Detroit.

1943

Timeline of WWII

- January 1 – German Panzer Division withdraws from the Terek River in southern Russia to prevent total encirclement.
- January 10 – Soviet troops launch an all out assault on Stalingrad.
- January 14 – At the Casablanca Conference, Churchill and Roosevelt discuss the eventual invasion of mainland Europe, along with Sicily and Italy.
- January 18 – The Jews in the Warsaw Ghetto start the uprising.
- January 23 – The Japanese continue their fight to hold western Guadalcanal; They have now given up on the New Guinea campaign.
- January 30 – The Japanese have escaped from Guadalcanal undetected. Hitler promotes general Paulus to Field Marshal and reminds him that no German Field Marshall has ever surrendered or been captured..
- January 31 – One day after his promotion, Paulus and his

staff surrender to Soviet troops in Stalingrad.

- February 7 – Shoe rationing will go into effect in the United States.

- February 9 – Guadalcanal if finally secured becoming the first major achievement in the Pacific war. Munich, Vienna and Berlin are bombed.

- February 11 – General Eisenhower is named supreme commander of the Allied armies in Europe.

- February 21 – American troops take the Russell Islands of the Solomon chain.

- March 2 – U.S. and Australian naval forces within three days sink eight Japanese troop transports during the Battle of the Bismarck Sea.

- March 6 – Rommel is forced to retreat from Tunisia. It will be his last battle in Africa.

- March 11 – The German army enters Kharkov as the fierce battle with Soviet troops continue. It is captured three days later.

- March 16 – For the ninth time, Stalin demands a "Second Front" and accuses the allies of treachery.

- March 23-26 – Patton's tank force defeat the Germans at El Guettar, Tunisia and the British break through the Mareth line in Southern Tunisia. The entire German army moves north to avoid entrapment.

- April 4 – Ten American POWs break out of the Davao Penal Colony and tell of the infamous Bataan death march and other atrocities of the Japanese.

- April 18 – Admiral Yamamoto is killed when his surveillance plane is shot down by American P38's over Bougainvillle.

- April 19 – In occupied Belgium, partisans attack a railway convoy transporting Jews to Auschwitz and 236 Jews escape.

- April 26 – The British take "Longstop Hill" in Tunisia, a key breakout route.

- April 30 – Lt. Jewell's crew release a body bearing false documents near the Spanish coast during "Operation Mincemeat". These fake documents will go on to mislead the Germans about the planned invasion of Sicily.

- May 11 – American and Canadian troops invade Attu Island in the Aleutian Islands in an attempt to drive out occupying Japanese forces.

- May 13 – The Allied forces in North Africa capture over 250,000 German and Italian forces in North Africa.

- May 16 – The Warsaw uprising ends with the killing of about 14,000 Jews and 40,000 Jews sent to death camps at Majdanek and Treblinka.

- May 22 – Allies bomb Sicily and Sardinia, both possible

landing sites.

- May 24 – Joseph Mengle (Angel of Death) is named Chief Medical Officer in Auschwitz.
- May 30 – Attu Island is once again under American control.
- June 13 – U.S. aircraft suffer heavy losses over Kiel.
- June 23 – American troops land at the Trobriand Islands close to New Guinea. The American strategy of driving the Japanese out of the Southwest Pacific by inland hopping continues.
- July 7 – Walter Dornberger briefs Hitler on the V-2 rocket, who approves the project as top priority.
- July 10 – "Operation Husky", the Allied invasion of Sicily begins.
- July 12 – The largest tank battle in history takes place near Kursk. It is the pivotal battle of "Operation Citadel."
- July 22 – Patton's forces capture Palermo, Sicily.
- July 25 – Mussolini is arrested and relieved of his offices.
- August 6 – German forces begin pouring over the Italian border to take over Italian defenses.
- August 11 – German and Italian forces begin to evacuate Sicily.
- August 17 – The RAF under "Operation Hydra", bombs the Peenemunde V-2 rocket facility.

- August 23 – Kharkov, Ukraine is liberated becoming the first major success of the Soviets summer offensive.

- September 3 – A secret armistice is signed and Italy drops out of the war. Nazi Germany begins the evacuation of civilians from Berlin.

- September 10 – German troops occupy Rome.

- September 12 – Mussolini is rescued by aircraft from his mountaintop captivity by German SS troops. Hitler remains loyal to his old friend.

- September 16 – After a German counteroffensive at Salerno, British and American troops link up near the Salerno beachhead.

- September 28 – The people of Naples, sensing the approach of the allies, rise up against the German occupiers.

- October 10 – Chiang Kai-shek takes the oath of office as chairman of Nationalist Government of China.

- October 13 – Italy, under a new administration, declares war on Germany.

- October 19 – The German War Office contracts the Mittelwerk to produce 12,000 V2 rockets.

- November 1 – "Operation Goodtime" has U.S. marines landing on Bougainville in the Solomon Islands. The fighting will continue until the end of the war.

- November 6 – The Red Army liberates the city of Kiev.
- November 14 – Heavy bombers hit Tarawa in the Gilbert Islands.
- November 15 – Allied Expeditionary Force for the invasion of Europe is officially formed.
- November 20 – Americans are shocked at the heavy loss of life on Tarawa as the marines land on the island.
- November 22 – At the Cairo Conference, president Roosevelt, Prime Minister Churchill and ROC leader Chiang Kai-shek discuss ways to defeat Japan.
- November 24 – For the second consecutive day, heavy bombing of Berlin continues.
- November 28 – At the Tehran Conference, Roosevelt, Churchill and Stalin meet to discuss the war strategy. By November 30, the establish an agreement concerning the June 1944 invasion of Europe to be called "Operation Overlord".
- December 12 – Rommel is appointed chief planner against the expected invasion of Europe.
- December 26 - German battleship, Scharnhorst, is sunk by the battleship HMS Duke of York.

ASA In 1943

In 1943, despite the armed forces' demand for more men, weapons, and equipment during the war, the ASA grew, by allowing regional championships. Because of the tremendous drain on manpower, many civilian teams had to suspend play, as sometimes entire teams were called into duty. Defense plants formed softball teams on a large scale, thus helping to offset the loss of civilian teams. The gigantic service program was a boon for softball.

Fast pitch was still the game of choice and service teams were eager to participate in the ASA Men's Major Fast-Pitch National Championship games.

Armed forces' service teams would participate and be very competitive until the late 1960's. This would include women's service teams as well. The renowned Hammer Field Raiders of Fresno, California would win the Men's National Championship in 1943 and 1944. They would be the only service team to win the championship.

Coca-Cola would be a huge help financially in 1943 after Pepsi-Cola dropped its sponsorship. Promotions manager, William Kaliska, donated more than $10,000 to buy trophies and help with office postage, and then an additional $5,000 for office operations. The Morrison Hotel donated office space and Johnson's newspaper paid his own expenses.

Financially, 1943, was a bad year for ASA, as the organization suffered through budgeting problems and was $12,132.47 in the red. The ASA would now owe secretary Pauley $10,330.85 after $1,470. 30 was added to the three previous years. The 1943 National Championship Tournament reflected a net loss of $4,080.97.

ASA president, Raymond Johnson, helped to convince Coca-Cola to provide trophies to all tournament winners, including national, regional, state, metro, industrial, junior, high-school and service tournaments. Johnson would explain this at the Spring Commissioners' Meeting on April 10, 1943 at the Medinah Athletic Club in Chicago. All of these awards were to be presented by the affiliated associations of the ASA through their regular appointed commissioners.

The Hammer Field Raiders almost didn't play in the National Championship tournament in Detroit. After winning numerous games in the San Joaquin Valley and San Francisco Bay Region, with two outstanding pitchers; Al Linde and Sargent Kermit Lynch, who pitched the team to the Pacific Coast Regional, being a service team, they needed to get permission to play in the National Tournament from officials in Washington D.C.

Once they obtained the difficult permission, they then faced the problem of finding a sponsor for their transportation to Detroit. The Hammer Field Officers' Club came through with $2,500 to pay the travel expenses. If this wouldn't have happened a "Minute

Man" Committee of local patriotic Fresnans were ready to step forward and pay the cost.

All of this adversity paid off, as the team prevailed over the Detroit Briggs Beautyware Bombers, 1-0, thanks to the brilliant pitching of Lynch, before over 5,000 fans at U of D stadium. Lynch also got the only hit of the game for Hammer Field a triple to drive in the only run of the game off Ed Pearl.

Briggs Bombers had an outstanding tournament behind the pitching of Ed Figelski, who opened with a 14 inning no-hitter with 27 strikeouts and then pitched a 4-0 shutout with 10 strikeouts, over Hammer Field to force another game for the Championship.

MVP: Kermit Lynch, Hammer Field Raiders

Batting Leader: Ed "Tyranski" Tyson, Briggs Bombers, 9 for 19, .473 average

The Jax Brewer Maids from New Orleans went undefeated to win the Women's National Championship. They collected 17 hits in their 7-0 win over the Arizona Ramblers from Phoenix. All of the players work for their sponsor with most doing clerical work and one is also a chemist for the firm. Nina Korgan tossed a one-hitter with nine strikeouts in the championship game and also went 2 for 4 with two RBI's. She was helped by Olympia Savona (2-3 and 2 runs scored) and Freda Savona (3-3 and 2 RBI's). Teammate Lottie Johnson also tossed a 6-0 no-hitter in the tourney. Amy Peralta of Phoenix took the loss.

Strangely enough, they were offered $65 to well over $100 a week to play in the newly formed All American Girls baseball league. All fifteen players refused, because they didn't want to break up their team. During the height of the war, women's professional baseball took off and Besides the AAGPBL, other girls baseball leagues formed.

Unofficial MVP: Nina Korgan, Jax Maids, (4-0, 54 K, 3 shutouts)

Batting Leader: Freda Savona, Jax Maids, (7-15, 6 runs, 6 RBIs, 2 HR, .467 Avg)

Numerous men's and women's teams could not participate for various reasons. The men's teams from Puerto Rico and Mexico did not attend due to WWII transportation restrictions.

ASA Softball of Michigan - 1943

The ASA Softball of Michigan was officially formed in 1943. The name would take the place of Michigan Softball Association which began in 1934. The official name would change again to Michigan Amateur Softball Association (MASA).

As the war progressed and the need to have multiple invasions and fronts in Europe, Pacific theatre, and Africa, there was a greater need for more men and even women. Softball In Michigan experienced a change from the competitive Game to one of just fun and recreation. Older aged men, not needed for the draft and women formed numerous industrial teams and played in an industrial league. The leagues sprung up all over the state, but due to restricted travel and rationing of gas, the players stayed closer to home and formed many local teams.

In 1943 and 1944, statewide tournaments were held in only the major and Class A divisions. The lower classes conducted tournaments more focused on the local "factory" tournaments. There were still district tournaments held for those who pursued the right to go to the state tournament in Lansing.

The Midland Dow Athletic Club (A.C.) once again won the men's major state championship and Andy's Service of Ferndale won the Class A division. In the women's division, Don McCullagh of Lansing won the major championship while Norge, from Muskegon won the Class A crown.

The Dow A.C. team formed in 1938 as the Chemical City Athletic Club before changing the name to the Midland Dow A.C. during the war. They would continue until 1955, after winning several state titles, three regional champions and two world titles. Famous players such as Al Linde, Jack Kett, and Dick Dudzik played on the team which was coached by Jimmy Walsh.

CHAPTER SIX
WWII, AND SOFTBALL CHANGES

1944

Timeline of WWII Events

- January 4 – The Red Army enters Poland as their front begins.

- January 20 – The RAF drops over 2,300 tons of bombs on Berlin

- January 24 – The Allied forces suffer a major setback on the Gari River in Italy. The effort to breakout from southern Italy would last until late May.

- January 27 – The siege of Leningrad ends after 872 days, as German forces withdraw. About two million died, mostly from starvation and disease.

- January 30 – At Anzio, Italy four battalions of Darby's Rangers would attempt to breakout from the beachhead. One battalion had only six men return out of 767 men. The rest were either killed, wounded or captured.

- February 2 – German troops defeat the American troops at the battle of Cisterna near Anzio.

- February 4 – The world's largest atoll, Kwajalein, a major Japanese naval base is now secured by the Allied forces.

- February 16 – German forces launch a major counterattack at Anzio, threatening to overtake the American beachhead.

- February 18 – The light cruiser, HMS Penelope, is torpedoed and sunk off the coast of Anzio with a loss of 415 crewmen.

- February 26 – A week long bombing begins on industrial cities in Germany.

- March 3 – After failing to drive the Allies out of Anzio, German forces now use defensive positioning.

- March 8 – The Red Army finally forces German troops into a major retreat in the Ukraine.

- March 28 – Japanese forces are in a major retreat in Burma.

- April 4 – General Charles de Gaulle takes command of all Free French forces.

- April 16 – Soviet forces take Yalta, most of Crimea has been liberated.

- April 17 – The Japanese using over 600,000 men launch "Operation Ichigo" in central China.

- April 27 – Hundreds of American sailors and soldiers are killed over two days during training exercises at Slapton, in preparation of D-Day.

- May 6 – Heavy bombing of the European continent in

preparation of D-Day.

- May 18 – The fourth battle of Monte Cassino ends in an Allied victory, as Polish troops led by general Wladyslaw Anders captures Monte Cassino.

- May 23 – Allied troops attempt a major breakout from Anzio beaches.

- May 25 – "Operation Horlicks" begins as Americans land on Biak, Dutch New Guinea, where a key Japanese air base is located.

- May 31 – The Japanese retreat from Imphal, India with heavy losses.

- June 4 – Allies enter Rome, one day after Germans declare it an open city.

- June 5 – Operation Overlord commences when more than 1,000 British bomber drop 5,000 tons of bombs on German gun batteries on Normandy beaches.

- June 6 – The long awaited Allied invasion occurs when 155,000 Allied troops land on Normandy beaches. It is the largest amphibious landing in history.

- June 12 – American carriers commence air strikes on the Marianas including Saipan, preparing for an invasion.

- June 13 – Germany launches V1 rocket attacks on England. Hitler views it as revenge for the Allied attack and believes his "secret weapon" will achieve victory.

- June 19 – The battle of the Philippine sea, called the "Great Marianas Turkey Shoot" takes place. Over 200 Japanese planes are shot down while only 29 American planes are lost.

- June 22 – London suffers heavy casualties from the V1 attacks. Soviet forces clear German forces from Belarus. One of the greatest defeats of the Wehrmacht during WWII.

- June 25 – The battle between Finnish and Soviet troops begins.

- June 27 – San Marino is bombed by the Allies, as the battle for Italy continues

- July 3 – The Allied armies are bogged down in Western France due to the huge hedgerows and the defense devices set up by the Germans.

- July 6 – 4,300 Japanese troops are slaughtered on Saipan due to the largest Banzai charge of the war.

- July 9 – Caen, France is liberated by British troops. Saipan is now secure.

- July 18 – General Tojo resigns as chief minister of the Japanese government as defeats of the Japanese military forces continue to mount.

- July 20 – The plot to assassinate Hitler fails when the bomb planted only wounds him. Reprisals follow against the plotters, their families, and even include Rommel.

- July 21 – US marines land on Guam.

- July 24 – Marines land on Tinian Island, last of the Marianas. It will become a B-29 bomber base and from which the Atomic bombers depart.

- August 4 – Florence and Rennes in France is liberated by the Allies. German general Albert Kesselring orders historic bridges and building destroyed.

- August 5 – Over 40,000 civilians are murdered by German and collaborating Soviet forces in the Wola district of Warsaw.

- August 9 – President Roosevelt approves general MacArthur's plan to invade the Philippines but turns down Admiral Nimitz's plan to invade Taiwan.

- August 14 – The Allies fail to close an escape route in France which allows Germans to escape the pincer movement of the Allies.

- August 22 – The Japanese are in total retreat from India. Hitler orders the German commander of Paris, general Von Choltitz to destroy the city.

- August 25 – General Von Choltitz disobeys Hitler's orders which allows Paris to be liberated. Charles de Gaulle makes a triumphant speech.

- August 28 – The Germans surrender at Toulan and Marseille in southern France. General Patton's tanks cross the Marne.

- September 2 – Allied troops enter Belgium.

- September 4 – A cease fire takes effect between Finland and Russia. "Operation Outward" ends.

- September 10 – Luxembourg is liberated by the U.S. First Army.

- September 13 – American troops reach the famed Siegfried Line, the west wall of Germany's defense system.

- September 15 – Marines land on Peleliu, this bloody battle will continue for over two months.

- September 17   "Operation Market Garden" begins as thousands of American paratroopers land in the Netherlands.

- September 22 – The Red Army takes Tallinn. The Germans surrender at Boulogne.

- September 23 – Americans take Ulithi atoll in the Caroline Islands. This huge atoll will later become an important naval base.

- September 25 – British troops pull out of Arnhem as "Operation Market Garden" is declared a failure. Over 80% of paratroopers suffer casualties.

- September 30 – Germans surrender at Calais to Canadian

troops. At one time this was going to be used by Hitler as a cross-channel invasion of England.

- October 2 – American troops are now in a full scale attack on the German 'West Wall".

- October 9 – Churchill and Stalin meet in Moscow to discuss spheres of influence in the Balkans.

- October 14 – Field Marshall Rommel commits suicide to save his family, as he was under suspicion as one of the Hitler's bomb plotters. He will be buried with full military honors.

- October 18 – Hitler orders a call-up of all remaining men from 16-60 for home defense in the Volkssturm Militia.

- October 20 – The battle of Leyte, Philippines begins. MacArthur lands and states, "I have returned".

- October 21 – Aachen, Germany is the first German city captured by the U.S. First Army.

- October 23-26 – During the battle of Leyte Gulf, the U.S. Third and Seventh Fleet win a decisive naval battle over the Japanese navy.

- November 2 – Canadian troops take Zeebrugge, Belgium. Belgium is now totally liberated.

- November 5 – U.S. planes bomb Singapore. The USS Lexington is heavily damaged by kamikaze attacks.

- November 10 – V-2 rockets strike Britain at the rate of about eight per day.

- November 20 – Hitler leaves his HQ at Rastenberg, East Prussia and will now reside in his bunker in Berlin.

- November 24 – The first B-29 bombers originating from Tinian, raids Tokyo.

- November 26 – Heinrich Himmler orders the gas chambers in Auschwitz and Birkenau dismantled and blown up.

- November 28 – Antwerp is now a major supply route for the Allies.

- December 8 – The bombing of Iwo Jima begins prior to the landing.

- December 14   The USS Ticonderoga strikes Japanese positions in Luzon, Philippines.

- December 16 – The Battle of the Bulge begins as German forces attempt a breakthrough in the Ardennes region.

- December 18 – Bastogne, an important crossroads is completely surrounded.

- December 20 – The 101st Airborne Division, surrounded in Bastogne are running low on all necessary supplies. German commanders demand a surrender which General Anthony McAuliffe answers, "Nuts!"

- December 23 – The sky is finally clear over the Ardennes

allowing Allied aircraft to begin their attacks on German forces.

- December 26 - The siege of Bastogne is broken by Patton's Third Army.
- December 29 – Soviet troops begin the siege of Budapest.

ASA During 1944

When the ASA Commissioners met in Cleveland, April 22-23, they faced a huge deficit. Commissioner James Rhodes of Columbus, Ohio was the chairman of the committee and their sole purpose was to figure out ways to pull the Association out of the red. Rhodes recommended that each team be assessed $2 in addition to their regular entry fee for membership fee charged by state or metro associations. The committee approved the plan and starting with the district tournaments began assessing the one time fee.

Secretary Pauley proposed the idea of selling ten sustaining memberships at $25 per year, the commissioners could raise another $4,000. His plan was also approved.

Elks stadium in Cleveland would be hosting the ASA National Championship this year and they would host for five years until 1948. The Lakewood Elks Club would underwrite the tournament and they provided a well lighted field, a cover for the grandstand and bleachers, an electric scoreboard and public address system.

Photo of the crowd at Elks stadium watching the
championship game

Playing night softball wasn't readily accepted by the neighboring community as they sued the club claiming that night softball would be a nuisance. A judge disagreed and threw the case out, claiming night softball was good entertainment provided there was a reasonable curfew. Elks stadium existed until 1958, when it was shut down and replaced by a chain store in 1959.

The Hammer Field Raiders from Fresno, California repeated as ASA National Champions in 1944. Al Linde and Kermit Lynch once again were the star pitchers. They beat a well determined Zollner Pistons team from Fort Wayne, Indiana 1-0. "The greatest thrill of his career. " Linde said.

Linde put on an outstanding tournament pitching 41 innings, winning all four of his games by shutouts and two of those were no hitters. He was 37 – 1 on the season with 15 no hitters. He was outstanding at the bat as he had two game ending walk off hits.

MVP – Al Linde – 21 strikeouts and a 1 – 0 shutout in championship game.

Lind & Pomeroy Florist from Portland Oregon dominated the women's tournament as they went 5 – 0 and all games were shutouts. They outscored their opponents 27 – 0. They were forced to play 11 innings to beat the Arizona Ramblers 1 – 0. Nira Deputy, went 3 for 5, singled home Dottie Moore for the win. Alyse Johnson and Betty Evans were the pitchers of record for the team.

Team photo of Lind & Pomeroy Florists Championship Team.

Two-time defending champion, Jax Maids lost two straight, both in extra innings. First to the Erin Brews of Cleveland, 1 – 0, in 14 innings and then to the Ramblers, 1 – 0, in 8 innings. During the season they played 40 games against men's military base teams, going 35 -5, finishing with a record of 44-8. The team was inducted into the Oregon Sports Hall of Fame in 1985.

The ASA began to see a financial turnaround in 1944, when the World's Tournament netted a profit of $4,366.20 with the East Central Region profiting $2,307.34. The Lakewood Athletic Commission assigned half this amount ($1,153.67) to pay for balls, bats, and umpire fees, then submitted the remainder to the ASA national treasury.

Because the war was escalating quickly, the year prior baseball began to see a major drop in their sport, as minor league parks began to suffer to even field a team. Philip K. Wrigley, who inherited the Chicago Cubs Major League team from his father, searched for a possible solution to the problem. He asked Ken Sells, assistant to the General Manager to come up with ideas. The committee suggested a girls' professional league be established and prepare to go into Major League parks should attendance fall.

The All American Girls Softball League was formed in 1943 which later that year was changed to the All American Girls Baseball League. By 1944 this became the All American Girls Professional Baseball League (AAGPBL). The sport immediately caught on and teams began wearing flashy satin uniforms and soon stadiums began filling up to watch their game.

Since the only organized ball for women was softball, a committee created a game which included both softball and baseball rules. Chicago and other urban cities also got semi-pro women's teams and used a 12 inch softball and underhand pitching. Before long base distances were extended allowing runners to lead off. The dilemma facing the new league was finding outstanding women's players willing to become professional players and jeopardize their amateur status. One of the first to sign was the famed catcher of the South Bend Blue Sox, Mary "Bonnie" Baker. She was featured on the cover of Life Magazine in 1945

Mary "Bonnie" Baker
© Life Magazine June 1945

Photo of Mary Baker

Bill Allington, former minor league player and coach, was an active scout for the AAGPBL. He later became coach of the Rockford Peaches in the summer of 1944 and remained in that capacity until the end of the league's existence. Wrigley attracted hundreds of players by using scouts and try outs in dozens of major cities. He envisioned that baseball parks could profit from having the women play on the dates the men's teams were scheduled out of town.

First players signed in 1943 Standing, L-R: Clara Schillace, Ann Harnett and Edie Perlick. Seated: Shirley Jameson. (From Northern

Photo of the first players signed in 1943

His idea was not well received so four non-Major League cities were selected that were in close proximity to the league headquarters in Chicago. These cities were Racine and Kenosha, Wisconsin, Rockford, Illinois, and South Bend, Indiana. A projected budget was developed and Wrigley agreed to fund half the cost of operating each team as well as over-budget expenses. Host city directors would fund the other half.

Players chosen, some as young as fifteen, were sent professional league contracts which stated they were not to have any other employment during the baseball season. Salaries were high, $45 - $85 a week, in many cases girls were making more money than their parents who had skilled occupations.

Players not only had to be highly skilled, they also had to abide with high moral standards and rules of conduct. Femininity was a high priority and Wrigley contracted with the Helena Rubenstein's Beauty Salon and the players had to attend evening charm school classes. In an effort to make each player as physically attractive as possible, each player received a beauty kid and instructions on how to use it.

Ann Harnett, Chicago softball star, became a model for the new uniforms which were one-piece short-skirted flared tunic fashioned after the figure skater, field hockey and tennis costumes of the time period. Satin shorts, knee-high baseball socks and baseball hat completed the uniform.

A schedule of 108 games was drawn up and the teams were well received as more than 176,000 fans turned out in their first season. Several factors played in to the success of the sport, as most of the nation was involved in the war effort and women left their homes to support the war by taking jobs in factories that were converted into making munitions and other military equipment.

May 14 to May 25, 1944 was the time set for the second spring training of the AAGPBL and it was held in Peru, Illinois. 120 girls, six managers, and league personnel were housed at either the Peru Hotel or the St. Francis Hotel in nearby LaSalle.

The Ruth Tiffany School was contracted to run the charm school at night. To encourage the need for a healthy mind and body, the arts of walking, sitting, speaking, selecting clothes, applying make-up and social skills were once again the main focus of attention. Wrigley, Paul Harper and Branch Rickey agreed to finance two additional teams to play in the league in their respective stadiums in Minneapolis and Milwaukee.

The women were excited to play in the larger stadiums in the big cities, however the drawback was the smaller cities newspapers reported on each game with even a box score while the major city newspapers barely mentioned them. Also the larger stadiums didn't allow for home runs like the smaller minor league parks.

By early summer of 1944, Wrigley began to lose interest in the league because of the poor attendance in the two major league parks. Overall attendance in the smaller cities increased but Wrigley sold the league to his Chicago advertising executive, Arthur Meyerhoff.

It was under his ownership that the league reached its peak. On November 15, 1944, he met with representatives from the four original cities and re-organized the league so each franchise would be governed by a Board of Directors comprised of representatives from each team. Ken Sills resigned as league president and Max Carey became the new league president.

The following year the Milwaukee Chicks were picked up by Grand Rapids, Michigan and the Minneapolis Millerettes went to Fort Wayne, Indiana. The emphasis changed from "Charm school" to actual ball players. The teams would play exhibition games at thirteen army camps and veteran hospitals during the first five days of spring training. The players would visit the hospitals and talk to the wounded soldiers.

The AAGPBL would celebrate the end of WWII on August 14, 1945 at the ball park. The league now was now gaining a true following as by the year's end attendance reached 450,313.

Michigan Amateur Softball

Because Michigan was a large industrial state, producing cars, engines, and other major components, the plants had already been turned into making tanks, air craft, bomber, machine guns and carbines for the increasing need. With the United States on two major fronts, these plants began working around the clock to meet the demand of the military.

This also became a boom to softball as industrial teams were gaining teams and thousands of people in their surrounding area, would turn out to watch their games a lunch hour or after their shift ended. Chrysler Corporation in Detroit had 394 teams and thousands of players enjoying the game.

However, because of the war many diamonds weren't in use at night and the lack of civilians meant a downward trend in those types of recreational teams. The MAS state tournament would take place in Lansing once again and with only two classes of play for men and women divisions.

The Elks Pontiac team won the men's major division and Kings from Lansing won the A division. For the women, Voss's from Flint won the major division and the Bee Hive team from Grand Rapids won the A division.

1945 – World War II Ends

- January 6 – American B-29's bomb Tokyo again
- January 9 – Americans land on Luzon, Kamikaze attacks on the navy continue as Japan is desperate to keep Americans from attacking.
- January 13 – The Red Army begins its East Prussian offensive but meets heavy resistance from the German 3rd Panzer army.
- January 15 – Hitler and his mistress, Eva Braun are now living in an underground bunker within Berlin.

- January 17 – The Battle of the Bulge officially ends.
- January 25 – The U.S. Navy bombards Iwo Jima preparing for the invasion.
- January 27 – The Red Army liberates the Auschwitz concentration camp.
- January 31 – The Red Army crosses the Oder river and are now within fifty miles of Berlin.
- February 3 – The battle for Manila begins. Japanese soldiers begin murdering civilians.
- February 4 – Roosevelt, Churchill, and Stalin meet at Yalta. The main discussion is postwar spheres of influence (who will control what).
- February 13/14 – The allied air forces firebomb the German city of Dresden.
- February 16 – American naval vessels bombard Tokyo and Yokohama.
- February 23 – U.S. marines raise the American flag on Mount Suribachi on Iwo Jima.
- February 25 – U.S. B-29's use incendiary bombs on Tokyo.
- February 26 – After ten days of fighting, American and Filipino troops recapture Corregidor.
- March 7 – German troops fail to dynamite the Ludendorff bridge over the Rhine. The U.S. First Army captures the

bridge and begins crossing over.

- March 10 – Japanese Fu-Go balloon bombs slightly damage the Manhattan project Hanford Site in Washington State.
- March 11 – Nagoya, Japan is firebombed by hundreds of B-29's.
- March 16 – Iwo Jima is finally secured. It is the only Marine battle where the number of American casualties is larger than the enemies.
- March 19 – U.S. carrier forces bomb naval bases in Japan, Kobe, and Kure. The USS Franklin (CV-13) is hit by two bombs killing hundred of sailors.
- March 20 – Patton's troops capture Mainz, Germany.
- March 22-23 – U.S. and British forces cross the Rhine at Oppenheim. Germany is under attack from all sides.
- March 27 – The Western Allies slow their attack and allow the Red Army to take Berlin.
- March 29 – The Red Army enters Austria. The Allies take Frankfurt as the Germans are in general retreat all over the center of the country.
- March 31 – General Eisenhower broadcasts a demand for German Surrender.
- April 1 – U.S. troops begins the battle for Okinawa.
- April 7 – The Japanese battleship Yamato is sunk off the

coast of Okinawa.

- April 9 – The last two major German warships are destroyed by the RAF.

- April 10 – Buchenwald concentration camp is liberated by Patton's Army.

- April 12 – President Franklin Roosevelt dies suddenly. Harry S. Truman become president.

- April 15 – Bergen-Belsen concentration camp is liberated by British forces.

- April 23 – Hermann Goring sends a request to Hitler in his bunker asking to be Hitler's successor. Hitler is furious and strips him of his rank.

- April 24 – Himmler makes a secret surrender offer to the Allies provided the Red Army is not involved. The offer is rejected. Hitler order Himmler be shot when he hears of the betrayal on the 28th.

- April 28 – Heavily disguised Benito Mussolini and his wife are captured trying to escape to Switzerland. They are shot and hung upside down in Milan.

- April 29 – Dachau concentration camp is liberated by the 7th Army.

- April 30 – Hitler and Eva Braun are married in his bunker and then they both commit suicide. Joseph Goebbels is appointed Reich Chancellor.

- May 1 – Goebbels and his wife murders their children then commit suicide.
- May 2 – Soviet forces capture the Reichstag building and raise the Soviet flag. German general Helmuth Weidling surrenders Berlin to the Soviets.
- May 7 – Germany formally surrenders to the Allies in Rheims, France at 2:41 a.m. as general Alfred Jodi signs in place of Hermann Goring.
- May 8 – Germany surrenders to the Soviet Army as general Wilhelm Keitel signs for Germany.
- May 9-11 – Numerous German occupied countries are liberated.
- June 2 – The USS Ticonderoga strikes airfields on Kyusha, Japan.
- June 5 – The allies decide to divide Germany into four areas of control (American, French, British and Soviet).
- June 13 – Admiral Ota Minoru, along with thousands of his brigade commits ritual suicide for failing to defend Okinawa.
- June 15 – Osaka, Japan is bombed. The Japanese are in retreat in central China.
- June 26 – The United Nations Charter is signed in San

Francisco.

- July 5 – MacArthur declares that the Philippines are fully liberated.

- July 16 – The first test of a nuclear weapon takes place in Alamogordo, New Mexico.

- July 17 – The Potsdam conference takes place with Churchill, Stalin and Truman agreeing to insist upon the unconditional surrender of Japan.

- July 24 – Truman hints at the Potsdam Conference that the United States has nuclear weapons.

- July 26 – The Labour Party wins the British general election by a landslide. Clement Attlee replaces Churchill as Prime Minister and immediately flies to the Potsdam Conference.

- July 28 – Japanese battleships, Haruna and Ise are sunk by aircraft by the U.S. Task Force 38 while anchored in shallow water at Kure Naval Base.

- July 30 – After delivering the atomic material to Tinian, The USS Indianapolis is sunk and hundreds of men die over the next four days.

- July 31 – U.S. air attacks on the cities of Kobe and Nagoya.

- August 6 – The B-29 bomber "Enola Gay" drops the first atomic bomb "Little Boy" on Hiroshima.

- August 8 – The Soviet Union declares war on Japan and

invades Manchuria an hour later. Japanese have been evacuating in anticipation of this.

• August 9 – The B-29 bomber, "Bockscar" drops the second atomic bomb "Fat Man" on Nagasaki.

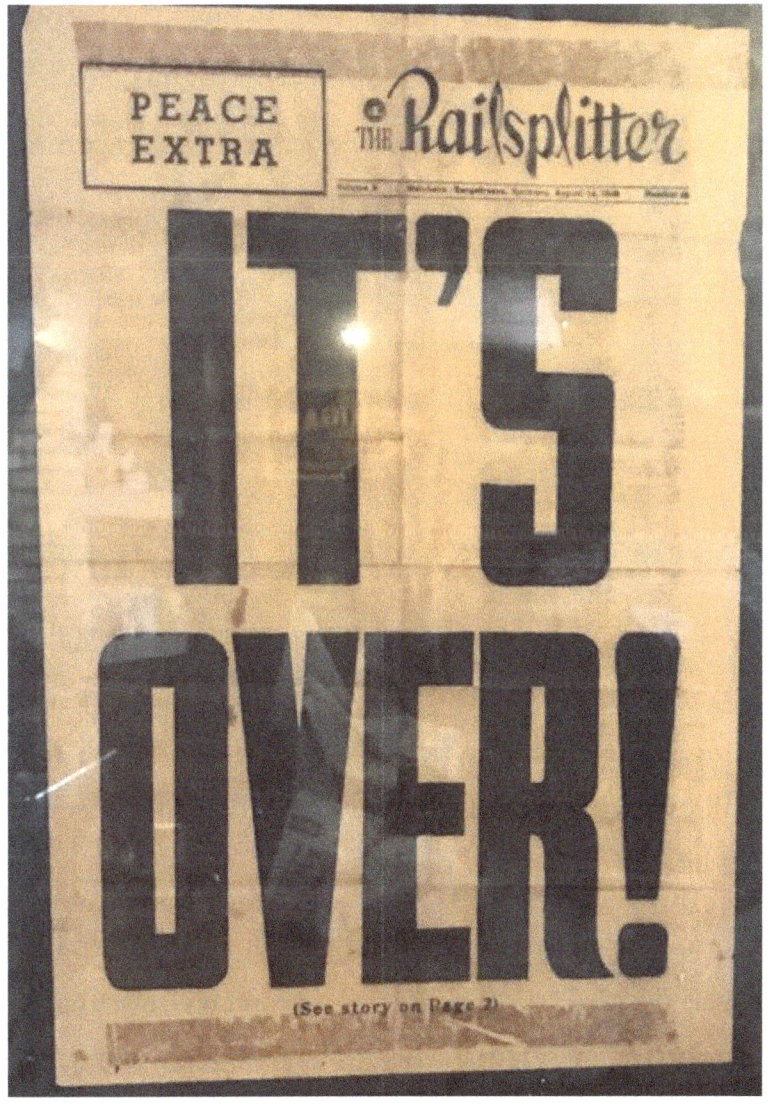

Photo of Newspaper Headlining "ITS OVER"

- August 15 – Emperor Hirohito announces the surrender of Japan. It seems to be unconditional, however, the Emperor's status is still open.

- August 19 – Ho Chi Minh occupies Hanoi, Vietnam and proclaims a provisional government. The French are in control of Vietnam south of the 16th Parallel.

- August 31 – General MacArthur takes command of the Japanese government in Tokyo.

- September 2 – The Japanese officially sign surrender papers on the deck of the USS Missouri.

- November 20 – The Nuremberg War Crimes Tribunal begins.

The ASA Thrives As The War Ends

As the Great War drew to a close, many changes were going to aid the ASA during the year. Hundreds of thousands of troops were going to be returning home and getting on with their lives and families. This would also mean a huge increase in leisure activities like softball, bowling, golf, etc.

The Commissioner's meeting was held February 3-4 in New York City. It was decided to split the job of secretary-treasurer, making each position independent of the other. Although Secretary Pauley didn't attend the meeting, he was in agreement of this proposal. Gus I. Kern of Cleveland was elected treasurer.

The Commissioners also voted that each state association be charged an additional fifty dollars in addition to the $100 affiliation fee, and that each Metro association be charged an additional $100 plus its $100 affiliation fee. This was needed to help payoff the Association debt of $10,330.85. In addition the umpire dues were raised to $3 with a dollar going back to the Association to which the umpire was a member of and $2 going to the national office.

The date of the annual meeting was changed to the last week of January or the first week of February in the future. Also, it was to be held in the same city that was scheduled to host the Sporting Goods Dealers Convention.

The ASA approved an Industrial World's Championship Invitational Tournament, with an entry fee of $100. ASA president Johnson appointed an eight men to run the tournament, which was to allow no more than four teams from any state association and no more than two teams from a metro association. A total of seven teams played in the inaugural even with the Briggs Bombers from Detroit beating the Zollner Pistons from Fort Wayne, Indiana. A total of $700 was raised for the ASA treasurer.

"Despite the war, and the unsettling conditions, the ASA enjoyed a successful season in 1945, just as it did throughout the war years", stated President Johnson. The total teams in the United States, Canada and Mexico were approximately 600,000, a staggering number considering the circumstances.

When the German's finally surrendered and the European Theatre was coming to an end, the army corps of engineers, which normally built bridges and airfields, began changing battlefields into ball fields. Shortly after V-E Day, the War Department in Washington, D.C., made available; 85,964 ball gloves, 72,850 baseballs and softballs, and 131,130 bats.

By mid-summer of 1945, 200,000 troops were playing in competitive leagues, military duties were sometimes scheduled around games and combat units temporarily put aside the emotional and physical scars of recent battles in their pursuit to be the best team on the base or in the region. Even the POW's took part in the game. Roger Long, of New Market, Iowa, who was a POW for 27 months, told writer Jan Castle Renander, "We played a lot of cards, I read the Bible from front to back and we made our own softball out of an unraveled sock. You can do anything if you set your mind to it."

In the 1945 ASA Guide, President Johnson wrote, "Frank Maxwell, a German prison camp POW, told of a group of Americans in the same camp with him making a ball and bat by hand in order that they might get to play. We found softball was the best thing possible in order to get our minds off our troubles being prisoners."

Johnson, who became the longest sitting President of ASA (1942-48) and who many thought was the savior of the game through the war, credited the commissioners, "Who did a wonderful job."

He also credited Coca-Cola for their contributions to the sport. "The Coca-Cola people were wonderful to us from the first time I mentioned the possibility of Coca-Cola sponsoring softball to the late Bill Kaliska (Coca-Cola promotions director) in December of 1942."

Elks Stadium in Cleveland would once again host the ASA World Championship Tournament. The crowds were even larger than the previous year, probably due to the complete ecstasy Americans were experiencing because the war had finally drew to a close. Softball needed America and America needed softball once again.

The Jax Maids, from New Orleans would once again be crowned World's Champs after missing out in 1944. They went undefeated (5-0) and didn't give up a hit until the third game. The Jax Maids beat the Crofton AC team from Toronto, Ontario Canada. The Maids were led by hitting stars, Dot Pitts and Dot Walker, each with two RBIs while the Savona sisters, Freda and Olympia each had two hits, accounting for 3 of the 5 runs scored. They shutout the Crofton AC team, 5-0.

Lottie Jackson, was 2-0 and also pitched a no-hitter, and struck out ten in 13 innings pitched. Nina Korgan was named the unofficial MVP as she went 3-0, one save, three shutouts, a no-hitter, 28 strikeouts in 22 innings pitched and was one for two in the final game.

1945 GIRLS' WORLD SOFTBALL CHAMPIONS

JAX GIRLS OF NEW ORLEANS—Front Row: Lechner, Pembo, Korgan, Bat Boy, Jackson, Meinecke, Camoa. Back Row: Brehm, trainer, Savona, Tillette, Walker, Cheron, Gill, Savona, Daul, Ragas, Pitts, Pailet, chaperon. Pailet, ASA Commissioner.

Photos of Jax Maids

The Men's Major Division was won by the Zollner Pistons from Fort Wayne (72-4 regular season) as they edged out the M&S Orange Beverage Company from Flint, Michigan (50-7) by a 1-0 score after losing the championship game prior by an identical score of 1-0. The famed Charlie Justice outdueled Zollner's Dizzy Kirkendale in the first final game, with Justice scoring the winning run, then Justice ran into some tough luck as his brilliant pitching ended when Chick Goldberg's base hit scored Neal Barille with the winning run.

Hughie Johnston of Zollner's went 6-22, .273 average, three doubles, three runs and six RBIs. Some newspaper said he was the MVP but it was the overall performance by Justice that was too much to ignore. Justice lost the first game of the tournament to Zollner's 3-2 then pitched seven consecutive shutouts. All total he gave up just four runs in nine games and had a streak of 55 scoreless innings. In one game against the Tip Top Tailers, he hurled a 19 inning 1-0 win as Bill Pack hit a home run to win the game. An astounding record for Charles Justice.

Michigan Amateur Softball

Everything didn't return to normal just because the war ended. The troops didn't all return home at once. The United States was an occupied force in two separate countries, Germany and Japan, and a substantial amount of troops were needed to allow this to run smoothly. The Islands in the Pacific still had enemy troops entrenched and fighting because they never got the word.

Commissioners met in late January to discuss the future and trying to return the state tournament to normalcy. One big rule change was made which eliminated the 10th player in the game of fast pitch and only nine players would now be needed.

This year the Men's Fast Pitch State Tournament would have three classes of play rather than just two as in the previous two years. M&S from Flint would be champions of the Major Division, A.C. Local 651 from Flint won the A Division and Macks A.C. of Ann Arbor won the B Division.

The Women's Fast Pitch State Tournament would also have

three classes of play with the Don McCullagh team from Lansing winning the Major Division, Nash Local from Lansing won the A Division and United Steel of Battle Creek winning the B Division.

Matt Urban, Most Decorated WWII Soldier

With the war finally behind us the need to mention Matt Urban, at this time is very apparent. Although not a Michigan native when he entered the war, He became a strategic part of the Michigan Softball Association program after the war as he eventually was named the state Commissioner in 1960. He also served as ASA national vice president for five years, on the executive board for five years and on most of the top ASA national committees.

Photo of Matt Urban with Congressional Medal of Honor

His heroism during the European Campaign is nothing short of miraculous. Lt. Colonel Steven W. Springer of Danbury, Connecticut, wrote, "In my opinion he was the greatest combat soldier ever. It was only God's will and guidance that extended and preserved this man's life in so many occasions." He was presented with 29 medals and awards for bravery during his 20 months of service.

Matt Urban was born in Buffalo, New York, on August 25, 1919, just after WWI ended. He excelled at numerous sports, particularly boxing, and dreamed of a career as a coach. He graduated from Cornell University and while there, he joined the Reserve Officer Training Corps and was an early draftee.

His first assignment was as Morale and Special Services Officer with the 9th Infantry Division, which was to participate in the invasion of North Africa in November, 1942. Urban was ordered to remain on board the ship and prepare for entertainment for troops returning from battle. Upon hearing of heavy resistance being met on the beach, Urban defied his orders and rowed himself to shore in a rubber raft to participate in the battle. His commanding officer had threatened him with a court martial for disobeying orders but he insisted that his rightful place was at the side of his friends. Upon reaching the beach, Urban replaced a wounded platoon leader and was promoted to executive officer of the 2nd Battalion for his exploits.

By March, 1943, U.S. forces had advanced to Tunisia where

German troops were trapped. Attempting to breakout, German troops attacked U.S. positions in the vicinity of the Kasserine Pass. Urban distinguished himself by knocking out a German observation post single-handedly and then leading F Company in a successful frontal assault on a strong enemy position. He suffered injuries to his hand and arm during these operations. For his efforts, Urban received two Silver Stars, a Bronze Star and two Purple Hearts.

Following the Allied victory in North Africa, the 9th Division was shifted to Britain in preparation for the invasion of Normandy. On June 14, 1944, Urban's unit became in an engagement near the town of Renouf, France, just inland from Utah Beach. During this fight, Urban used a bazooka to destroy a German tank and suffered a severe injury to his left leg. The following day he was shot through the right forearm, and was evacuated to England to recuperate.

While confined to a hospital, Urban read a newspaper account of his unit's exploits near the town of St. Lo, France. When he heard of that the 2nd battalion had suffered heavy casualties, he discharged himself from the hospital and made his way to the front, still limping from his leg wound. Urban was immediately involved in a furious firefight.

With the 2nd Battalion pinned down by heavy artillery fire and threatened with encirclement. Urban led his force forward, helped man a tank that suffered loss of a crew, and eventually brought the battalion to safety. Shortly after the battle, the commander of the 2nd Battalion was killed, and Urban was promoted to become his replacement. He was wounded by shrapnel in the lower back and chest.

Urban refused hospitalization to remain in action with his unit. Marveling at his ability to return to action after being wounded, Urban's fellow soldiers nicknamed him "The Ghost". Although the men were frozen and paralyzed, Buck Johnson of the Chattanooga Times later wrote, "Urban screamed at them to get on their feet, gave us back our confidence and he actually saved our lives."

The Allied forces broke out of the Normandy Peninsula during the summer of 1944 and raced across France, Belgium, Luxembourg and into Belgium. By September, Urban and his unit were involved in fighting in the vicinity of Philippeville, Belgium. As the 2nd Battalion attacked German defensive positions, Urban's troops were pinned down so he tried to get to one of his patrols pinned down at the foot of a machine gun nest.

Running and ducking to avoid being hit, he threw two grenades at the emplacement. It was then that Urban suffered his most serious injuries, as a bullet ripped through his throat, spinning him around. Both holes spurted blood like a fountain. "I said a thousand prayers in a few seconds", Urban recalled.

Two enlisted men, Private Schekt, an Austrian by birth and his interpreter, and an Alabama private named Price crawled out to him. Schekt put a finger on each side of his neck to stop the flow of blood. Price crawled back, got a fountain pen and rammed it into the hole in Urban's neck, then the two brave men dragged their major by the ankles over the crest of the hill.

Major Norman Weinberg, of Cincinnati, performed surgical wonders under fire in a muddy ditch while the chaplain, who had crawled through the mud, administered the last rites. Rough, tough GI's gathered around, nearly all were openly crying. They were sure their leader was too tough to die. He suffered permanent damage to his vocal chords and by the time he recovered the war had ended and he was released in February, 1946

A colonel and a staff sargeant, who had witnessed Urban returning to battle, had filled out paperwork recommending Urban be awarded the Congressional Medal of Honor. Unfortunately the colonel was killed shortly thereafter and the paperwork was lost in the Army bureaucracy where it would remain for more than 35 years.

A reporter conducting research on Urban's military service in the late 1970's discovered the lost Medal of Honor recommendations. The Army began their search for witnesses finally concluded the worthiness for the Medal of Honor. It was then they found the seventh Purple Heart, the Legion of Merit, and the Croix de Guerre that Urban never received. President Jimmy Carter presented Matt Urban with the award on July 19, 1980.

After leaving the Army, Urban became a writer on veteran's affairs for "Liberty Magazine". After three years, he became the recreation director for the city of Port Huron, Michigan. He held that position until 1956 before serving as the director of the Monroe, Michigan community center for 16 years, before becoming the director of the Holland, Michigan civic center and recreation director in 1972

A devoted softball player and enthusiast, he was known around Holland as "Mr. Softball". Matt Urban died on March 4, 1995 in Holland and is buried in Arlington Cemetery in Arlington, Virginia. The city of Holland named a public park and recreation complex in his honor later that year.

PART

II

PART TWO

THE LEGACY OF BILL HUMPHREY

Chapter Seven

The Early Years

When does a legacy begin? Is it when a person's touch on an organization begins? Perhaps it's when its ended and all the accolades and accomplishment are noted and recorded? Rather still, is it when a person takes an interest in an organization in his early years? This was the task before me as I took notes and gathered information as I sat with Bill Humphrey for hours on end. Let's begin.

Bill Humphrey was introduced to the game of fast pitch softball when Buck Sweebe, a player for the Stearns team in Midland, Michigan, accidentally hit young Bill over the eye while he was near the on deck circle on. Bill was just six years old. His dad took him to the ball field so he could be the bat boy. That is quite an introduction to the game of fast pitch. He was hooked.

"I wasn't hurt just surprised but needless to say I wasn't allowed anywhere near the on deck batter again," Bill said.

Born on March 18, 1939 to Mary Alice (Boyd) and Alva

Otho Humphrey. His grandfather's name was Haskell Hayford Humphrey of Welsh/Wales descent. He had an older sister, Mildred (Millie), born in 1933, and an older brother, Roger, born three years prior to Bill. Another brother was born but died at birth. When just six months old, his dad built a house on 161 Arbury Street, where they resided for many years.

Bill's dad played softball, bowled, and umpired in the top fast pitch league in the city. He took Bill to many a game, especially when he was about ten years old. Bill enjoyed being in the bullpen. "I got to know the famed Dow A.C.'s really well as I played catch with some of the best, Bill Barryman (nickname Booger), Bill Gorley, John Skalnicky, Clyde Dexter, and Bob Baker who were all pitchers. Bobby Wright was the catcher and he would give me tips on what they were throwing.'

With a vacant field across the street from his house and 4-5 boys in the neighborhood, it was easy to get a pick up baseball game started. Before long a few more boys would join in. Dow would sponsor youth baseball teams through the Athletic Club by working with schools in the area with 4th. 5th, and 6th grades. There were four sports; baseball, basketball, football, and softball.

Bill attended the State Street school and he played in a league administered by the schools. They were known as the "Tuffies" Our rival was St. Bridges, and one time during the football season, Bill had to stay after school for some disciplinary action. The "big game" was that afternoon and he wasn't going to miss playing.

When the teacher left the classroom, Hubby Waite and Bill jumped out of the window about one and a half stories, played the game then returned. Of course they were caught and now had to stay after for two days.

Dow sponsored some little league teams and Bill played for Les Myers in 1951. Williamsport, Pennsylvania was becoming famous for hosting the Little League World Series since its inception in 1947 and Bill was the right age (12) to play. Other cities were holding tournaments around the country to send teams, Escanaba hosted a four team tournament. They were a great team and beat Bill's team to qualify for the LLWS.

Bill recalled that when he was just eleven years old, his little league team was playing in a tournament in La Fayette, Indiana. He said, "It felt like the big time, Wow, I'm staying in a motel room and I'm playing baseball."

1951 turned out to be a very tragic year for Bill. His father and mentor passed away suddenly, and there is nothing much worse for a twelve year old boy than to lose his father. Thankfully he had sports to get him through plus umpiring was getting in his blood.

His mother and sister would play a huge role after Bill's dad died, taking him to his games, keeping him involved in sports, etc. His sister Mildred, had to quit school and work to help support the family.

"I remember my first dance in my freshman year," Bill recalled.

"I didn't have anything nice to wear. Mildred bought me a sports coat, pants, a pink shirt, white buck shoes with actual pink soles! I was the 'cat's ass'!"

He was just thirteen when he was umpiring his first meaningful game. He remarked about a play where a grounder was hit to the shortstop and as he fired it to first base. He immediately thought, "Whoa, I have to make that call." All of my preparation and teaching from my dad kicked in. He was hooked. He didn't want to just play softball and baseball, he wanted to umpire also.

At the age of fourteen, He played Legion Baseball and he stayed with the same team for five years. "One time I got picked off first base. I got up and yelled 'Balk' " he recalled. "About a second later the umpire yelled "Balk" and I smiled on my way to second base."

Dow Chemical had an athletic club called the Dow AC which sponsored various sports in grade schools. They had a Junior A.C. program and grade school leagues were formed throughout the city. Famous softball players like Clyde Dexter would coach the teams. When Little League and Pee Wee Football grew across the country, Dow AC stopped sponsoring in 1955 due to that competition.

"I followed a comic strip character named Ozark Ike in the newspapers," Bill laughed about. "So we called our team the 'Bugs'."

Photo of Bill playing baseball

Central Intermediate School would be his real learning experience to prepare him to play high school sports. When attending Midland High School, he would play on a strong football team which lost just one game to Bay City Central. Bill would play center as a freshman for the basketball team which went undefeated. However, he really excelled at baseball.

Bill was an outstanding pitcher and outfielder and after high school he was offered a tryout with the Detroit Tigers in 1957.

Pat Mullins was the Tiger scout and Bill had a bad knee, but he didn't want it known. His strong arm made up for the bad knee and he was offered a minor league contract for $250. He thought, "Nobody can replace my dad" so he turned it down. Besides he wanted to go to college and get a degree which wouldn't happen if he played minor league baseball.

Bill attended Manchester College at N. Manchester, Indiana for two years. He stated that he wanted to play baseball "Before I flunked out, but I fooled them." When Bill was a little boy his family took him to the Michigan State University campus frequently.

Bill became one of the best players on the team while there.

He said he thought it was one of the prettiest campuses he ever saw. After graduating from Manchester College, Bill enrolled at MSU and he recalled that as he was walking across the football field one day, guy who remembered me from somewhere, yelled at him and asked if I was a trainer. That was the beginning of my first job which I held for six years.

Working four different jobs was difficult to say the least. Being a trainer for the freshman team and being able to be on the sidelines for home games by the Varsity team and helping some great players such as; Bubba Smith, George Webster and Gene Washington was truly a bonus. One of my "jobs" was umpiring and shall we say "real love" was just beginning.

ASA and MASA

After WWII and entering the 1950's major changes would be occurring for the ASA. Prior to the annual meeting in Chicago in 1949, M. J. Pauley would resign as ASA executive secretary after sixteen years of dedication. In a letter dated January 27, 1949, the day before the annual meeting, Pauley wrote, "My health can no longer stand the rigors of conducting the office."

Byron Eugene Martin, Eastern Vice President, was asked to step in as Pauley's successor. Although Pauley didn't attend the meeting, he agreed with the decision. Martin was the ASA treasurer, taking that job in 1946, when the ASA decided in 1945 to split the job of Secretary/Treasurer into two separate roles. Martin would continue to serve until his death on July 14, 1962, a victim of cancer at the age of fifty-six.

The long career of Pauley and his involvement in the growth of softball in America had come to an end. Being one of the two founding fathers of the Amateur Softball Association along with Leo Fischer which began in 1933. Pauley would pass away in September of 1952, just three years after resigning his position.

The year 1949 saw the ASA register the largest number of teams since its inception and also reached nearly 5,000 male umpires registered. The following year, Madeline P, Lortan from the Bronx, would register as the first female ASA umpire. It was also the year when ASA decided to hold the men's and women's fast pitch National Championships in two separate cities.

The Tip Top Tailors, from Toronto, won the men's championship in Little Rock, Arkansas led by pitcher Charlie Justice. The women's tournament was held in Portland, Oregon and the Arizona Ramblers would repeat as they captured the championship.

Perhaps the best news the ASA experienced in 1949 was that the financial Records would show its largest unencumbered balance. This would prompt the Commissioners Conference in Louisville, at its meeting in January of 1950 to establish a travel fund for teams. They also adopted a new constitution and by-laws, and approved the organization of national federations in various softball playing countries.

"From these national federations will come an International Softball Federation which will be the representative body of the nations in the Olympics and Pan American competition." Wrote president Nick Barack in the 1950 ASA Official Guide. " There is not much doubt that this plan will become a reality at an early date, and our boys and girls will have a privilege to represent their country in international competition."

The 1950's was a decade of maturity and innovation for ASA. Youth programs were started, the inception of the Hall of Fame, the development of the annual All-Star Fast Pitch Series for men and women, and the first National Softball Interpretation Clinic. It was also when the growth of slow pitch really took hold. It became the "people's sport" as anyone could play the game.

In 1951, an ASA survey showed 65,210 registered teams, 978,150 players and 8,153 registered leagues. The ASA also decided to hold the Men's and Women's Fast Pitch National Championships in Detroit to help celebrate the city's 250th anniversary. The ASA also nationally promoted its first "National Softball Week".

Fast Pitch softball still remained the most popular in the early 50's but by 1953 the ASA recognized the need to add slow pitch championship play for that fast growing game. It was called the World Softball Tournament and was held in Cincinnati. Twelve teams competed in the inaugural tournament won by Shield's Contractors from Shreveport, Kentucky.

The Men's Major Fast Pitch National Championships were dominated by Michigan teams in the early 50's. Midland Dow A.C. won in 1951, while Briggs Beautyware from Detroit would capture the title in 1952 and repeat in 1953.

Midland Dow A.C. National Champs

For the small town of Midland, winning the national title was huge. However, they had to play the famous Clearwater Bombers twice to accomplish it. John Hunter of the Bombers went 5-0 with 75 strikeouts, 39 innings pitched and three one-hitters before hurting a nerve in his pitching arm. In the winner bracket final, Hunter defeated Dow AC, 3-1 with 10 strikeouts. That win forced another game to be played for the National Championship as it was Dow's first loss. Clyde "Lefty" Dexter was the star pitcher for Dow AC, as he went 3-0 with 42 innings pitched with 36 strikeouts. Amazingly he tossed a complete game of 21 inning shutout ball against the Grumman Yankees from New York. Dexter also hit a grand slam homer to win the game and go to the championship game.

Photo of Dow AC team.

John Skolnicki pitched in the Championship game, winning a 10-0 shutout while also going 2 for 2 with a double and two RBI's, Al Linde was 11-28, .393 batting average, and went 3-4 in the Championship game with a home run, triple, three RBI's and two runs scored.

Dexter and Linde were named to the All-America team. Other Dow players were; Loren Dinkel, Don McDonald, Keith Allsweed, Jim Hall, John Shaffer, Bill

Corley, Bob Wright, Dick Dudzick, Bob Baker, Joe Glebovich, Jimmy Strieter, Jack Kett, and Jim Walsh was the manager of the team.

CHAPTER EIGHT

MASA Withdraws from the ASA

One of the strangest things to occur during the 1950's happened in 1956 involving the Michigan Amateur Softball Association and the Amateur Softball Association. After decades of close ties, MASA chose to withdraw from the ASA due to a change in policy. The previous year, 1955, 650-700 fast pitch teams were participating in MASA with quite a few competing for a national berth.

That policy required that all softball teams be required to join the ASA regardless of their classification. This didn't sit well with many Michigan teams, especially from the Upper Peninsula and northern part of the state, as they felt membership should be voluntary rather than mandatory. Also many major fast pitch sponsors, such as Dow Chemical and Briggs Beauty Ware were cutting back on cost of softball. It was therefore difficult to find many teams willing to participate in ASA national tournaments.

Bill Humphrey decides Umpiring is his "love".

The 1960's was a special decade in Bill's life. He realized that playing softball was not his true "love" nor was it providing an avenue for his true ability. "Going to bat against the great Bonnie Jones was a true eye opener." Playing against some of the best teams in the state was a thrill but obviously not for me.

I was attending Michigan State University at the time and holding down a job running the Rec League and playing softball. Our team, "The Bombers" didn't belong playing against one of the premier pitchers in the state. We would travel to Detroit on the weekends to play against the top teams. "Bonnie just didn't throw fast balls, he had a drop ball, a great change up and he could hit his spots. Wherever the catcher's glove was, you could bet the ball would be there."

"I was put into a game and was told I was batting 6th. My first at bat the first pitch was up and in. Bonnie sent me a message. However, I did manage to foul it off. I got back in the box and PHHHT," Bill motioned with his hand. "My three at bats were two ground outs and a pop up to the shortstop. Pretty good I might add but still no hits." I decided that would be my last game and would pursue umpiring instead. .

"When you make a commitment, every step you take, every word you speak, supports it."

Bill started umpiring at age 11 but really took it serious at thirteen years old and at age fifteen was getting $2 a game. His first state tournament was Little League at that age. That's quite an accomplishment for such a young man.

"My Little League state championship at 15 told me a lot, Bill said. "You go through what you think you know and what you thought you had, then you learn quickly that I didn't."

"I had a game when I was umpiring the men's Rec League, I threw the coach and the catcher out." Bill stated. When asked by the Rec Director, I said, "They both used the word 'Hell', so I tossed them." Bill laughed as he finished, "Years later, some guy, a red head, named Bob Utterback, was having a few beers, told me, 'a young whipper snapper threw me out for saying the word Hell'."

Of course the Rec Director wasn't happy with what Bill did, but the Superintendent of Midland Schools sent him a letter and congratulated him for upholding the integrity of the game.

Bill was holding down two jobs while he was umpiring at MSU. He was hired as the trainer by the football coach and he was also supervising the recreation program for the Lansing recreation department.

"I was walking near the football field one day and I heard someone yell 'Hey You' ", Bill recalled. "It was one of the MSU football coaches and he remembered me. He yelled out, 'You want a job?' That was how I became a trainer." I remember taping up Ron Johnson, George Webster, Bubba Smith and many other greats on the football team.

"In 1961, while running the recreation department in Lansing, I was attending a meeting in Midland and all of the 'Big Boys' around the state were there," Bill said. "I felt way out of place. I know these guys were wondering 'Who is this kid?' but I had a lot to offer.".

The Boulevard in Midland was a very popular bar/restaurant for players and umpires to hang out. Lansing didn't have a UIC but Midland had an "unofficial UIC" and many a time a "meeting" would occur and we would go over the rule book, section by section, Bill said. "More was accomplished during one of those sit downs than any organized meeting," Bill added.

One time there was all the "horses" at the "Bully", (the favorite nickname of the Boulevard). There was a mixture of six players and umpires and the discussion went to a play where a batter/runner backed up on the way to first base and how it should have been ruled. A $5 bet was made by Bill that they were all wrong. There was a few differences of opinion and Bill said, "If the batter/runner is being played on it is a dead ball, out, and all runners must return to the last base touched." Of course this was the correct rule but Bill didn't keep the money. He collected each bet and put the total in the middle of the table for drinks.

Flashing back to his umpiring days, Bill recalled some of his favorite come backs. "One of my favorites was when a young woman yelled, 'If you were my husband I would feed you poison.'" I turned around and said, "If you were my wife I would gladly drink it." "The crowd loved it, but I don't condone making comments to those making comments to umpires. You are just better off ignoring them."

Then Bill smiled and I could see that gleam in his eye as he recalled another one. "A little boy was behind the back stop and he kept sticking his fingers through the fence. I tried warning him a couple of time to no avail." Finally I went over and said, "If you get hit, it might cut your fingers off and then you won't be able to pick your nose." The crowd laughed but the boy went away crying. "At least it worked," Bill smiled as he said that.

"There is nothing natural about umpiring."

Marriage

1966 became a very important year in Bill's life. While working at Dow Chemical in Midland, Bill was assigned to the Dow International Division, which was responsible to for products going to all points of the world. Bill was in charge of products being sent to Africa. A certain Co-op student caught his eye. That student was Nancy.

It wasn't long before they started dating. One memorable date occurred during Memorial Day weekend when about twelve friends decided to go camping and golfing up north near Petosky. When Bill and Nancy left Midland it was about 76 degrees and beautiful. Michigan can be quite different "Up North" weatherwise even in late May. "That first night it got very cold and I went out and bought a heater," Bill stated. When morning came, it began to snow after we all started our round. By the 3rd hole I said "The Hell with this! I'm done."

Nancy and Bill were married on November 26, 1966 and recently celebrated their 55th anniversary. Now Dow International had a rule that a husband and wife couldn't work together in the same department. Nancy decided to take a transfer to Las Angeles and of course Bill went with her.

Photo of Bill and Nancy

One night, about eight months later, as Bill was returning home from work and was traveling south a semi-truck jackknifed and traffic was all tied up. Bill thought of a BBQ." This didn't happen. By the time he got home, the food prepared by Nancy was cold.

He decided that L.A. was not the place for a young man.

"How would you like to go home?" Bill asked Nancy.

"I don't have any vacation time," Nancy replied.

"I'm not talking about vacation," Bill added.

They packed their bags and headed back to Midland. The year was 1968 and Bill began his career as an insurance sales representative.

"I discovered I was a horrible insurance salesman but I was a pretty darn good umpire."

Bill recalled a trip to Disneyland while they were living in L.A. "The Three Little Pigs were at the entrance, a little boy walked up, stared at them, and then proceeded to kick each of them in the shins." That was my introduction the park. "Nancy and I went on the bob sled up the Matterhorn," he laughed as he said, "That was not my cup of tea, but the Pirates of the Caribbean ride really did it. When we came down and then blasted along, it was all over."

Bill also has two daughters, Kari, now a retired school teacher living in North Carolina and Lori living in the Detroit area.

1969 – MASA re-joins ASA

After 13 long years it was time to re-join the Amateur Softball Association. MASA would remain disassociated with ASA for 13 years before reinstating in 1969. State president Jim Woiderski, and first Vice-President Robert Carlin led the effort, in 1968, to reunite the Michigan Amateur Softball Association and the Amateur Softball Association into one organization. This was accomplished in 1969 thanks to the two organizations executive boards.

Matt Urban, MASA State Commissioner stated, "MASA had the teams and ASA had the big tournaments, so to better the thousands of fast and slow pitch teams, it was only good common sense to pull together as on organization." The merger allowed Urban to remain as State Commissioner and assist Walt Balcom with MASA secretary functions. Balcom became deputy State Commissioner under Urban

The 60's were tumultuous times not just for MASA but also the nation. The Vietnam war was demanding more young men so the draft was implemented, race riots broke out across the country, and the Hippy movement was taking hold. All of these affected ASA and MASA in regards to softball.

CHAPTER NINE

"TIME AND PLACE"

Bill Humphrey repeatedly stated that many of the fortunate things that happened in his life is because of "Time and Place". He would say, "I just happened to be in the right place at the right time."

This statement is true for many people in life, but in Bill's case he was the right person at the right time for MASA, and also for ASA.

After reuniting with ASA in 1969, MASA took on major responsibilities and changes in the 70's. There is nothing in the archives as to how ASA perceived MASA after pulling out of their organization.

In 1969, Matt Urban was the state commissioner, Walt Balcom was the deputy state commissioner under Urban, Bob Carlin was the new secretary/ treasurer, In 1971 ASA recognized the appointments of state and Metro UIC's.

"Walt Balcom was the man!" Bill emphatically stated. "Softball in Michigan would have been nothing without Walt. He was the all time, 'God' of softball."

Bill remembered umpiring with Tom Mason, one of the best on rules. "I was young, a little arrogant, and I told him he was wrong on a rule. I realized quickly what kind of umpire I would be because I worked at it. I would know the rules!"

"Don't put a rule in the book you know you can't enforce."

Ike Smith became the MASA state UIC in 1970 through 1973, but he had no program for how to develop umpires. Bill worked with Ike for six years before he realized he was the state UIC! Tom Mason, who was appointed ASA national UIC in 1972, conducted an umpire clinic in Flint, in 1972 which Bill attended. There was basically no local leadership in districts or areas across the state. This made it extremely difficult to accomplish any task which required someone in a leadership role to take the reins and formulate a group of people to get things done. This would quickly change under the leadership of Bill Humphrey.

This was also the first year that each state and metro association would have an umpire-in-chief. Also, eighteen would be the minimum age to be an umpire. Each state and metro area operates their own organization through a state or metro association affiliated with the ASA. A commissioner was appointed by the ASA to administer the ASA programs and activities in State and metro areas

The following year ASA dedicated the National Hall of Fame and Museum in Oklahoma City. Charles Justice became Michigan's second hall of fame player in 1974, following Al Linde of Midland who was inducted in 1958.

In 1974 during an executive board meeting, Bill, who was now the state UIC, suggested the idea of District UIC's. Umpires would be charged an additional $2 for training and development. The executive board turned down this proposal and when Bill proposed it again the following year, it was once again refused.

The ASA national office requested that Bill be assigned to umpire the Men's Major National Fast Pitch tournament in Haywood, California in 1975. "It took me 25 years of my umpire career, but I was ready," Bill emphasized.

ASA only held national Major fastpitch, women's major fastpitch, Men's major slow pitch and Women's Major slow pitch. To be selected as an umpire was difficult because of how few natonal tournaments were conducted.

"I was selected to two national tournaments in 1975, the Men's Modified Major in Port Huron, Michigan just a week prior to my Men's Major Fast Pitch in Haywood, California. The Modfied Major was trying to say the least, especially when I called three illegal pitches in a row to score the winning run in the bottom of the 7th inning against this one team whose coach told the UIC I didn't know the rules.

"Bill Findley was my UIC for Men's Major ASA tournament in Haywood, California," Bill recalled. "I was almost late for the 7:00 meeting. I opened the back door exactly at 7:00 and sat on the floor trying to hide. It worked. Six umpires were cut after the first round and I wasn't one of them. The next year it finally passed.

"I asked a question about how we were going to call the pitching rule but didn't get a response right away, so I asked again. Seeing Tom Mason in the room I was certain I would get an answer."

Findley replied, "By the book."

"My first game was a little humorous. I was the plate umpire and there was a line drive down the left field line in which I called foul. The coach yelled that he saw chalk. I told him to go down and look at the line. The foul lines were actually 2" X 6" boards placed in the dirt and painted white. The coach came back and sheepishly looked at me but never said a word."

"My third game I was at 1st base and I called a few illegal pitches which kind of set the tone. Quite a few umpires followed suit after that."

"Listen to me, I'm nothing without ASA!"

MASA hosted a Special Olympics tournament in the early 70**'s.** Bill was on the Board of Directors and he wanted to put a package together for Special Olympics softball. Marty McGuire would be heading this. The question came up about umpires and if they would be willing to umpire for free.

"We agreed to have the host pay, but the umpires decided to donate. I told the umpires at the beginning of the tournament that if there was ever a time to step up, this was it." Bill said.

"I umpired the first game behind the plate and threw the ball out to the pitcher," Bill laughed. "He turned and threw the ball out to center field. Now he's facing me and is wanting a game ball. I said, 'Hey pitch, that was the game ball.'"

"Why didn't you say so!" the pitcher yelled back.

"Now the catcher was just a little girl who had Down's Syndrome," Bill recalled. First pitch ball goes by to the backstop. Second pitch same thing. Third pitch, I dodge another one. It turns out her mask wouldn't fit and she couldn't see the ball. I had everything I could do to not laugh."

Bill says that she yells at the batter, "Hit that ball hard!"

The batter turns and shouts, "Don't tell me what to do."

This is how the game would go, and its why umpiring the Special Olympic games are so enjoyable. Central Michigan University was hosting the games and after opening ceremonies, Detroit Metro took over.

Later in the tournament, Bill was umpiring with Jack Sauder. A player didn't like Jack's call and kicked dirt on Jack's pants and shoes. Jack kicked dirt back. "I walked down and threw Jack out of the game and took over," Bill laughed as he finished. "Another time when umpiring with Rick Owen, a runner passed another runner and he refused to call him out. I said, 'You have to do it.' as we were moving back and forth between bases."

*As Bill and I talked I told him about my first experience umpiring Special Olympics softball. Don Newsted was the UIC and knew I had little experience umpiring slow pitch and this was my first game behind the plate. An entourage of umpires was sitting behind the backstop watching.

"I called a strike on a batter, and the batter turned and gave me the finger right in my face," I laughed as I recalled the incident. "I was taken back and of course did nothing even after he repeated it for the second and third time."

"That was the only time in my career that a player could get away with that and not get ejected." I stated. "I never enjoyed myself more than when I umpire in that tournament!"

"Time and Place"

Bill was given the opportunity to umpire the Men's All-Star Fast Pitch Series in 1976 at Allentown, Pennsylvania and also was selected to be the UIC for the Women's Major Fast Pitch in Allentown, Pennsylvania in the same year.

However, one of his first great selections was to the ASA national staff as deputy umpire-in-chief in 1977 at the young age of just 38. Once again **"Time and Place"**.

In 1977 Midland hosted their first Men's Major Fast Pitch National Tournament thanks to the efforts of the Midland Softball Association. They are now known as the "Red Coats" after they all wore red warm up jackets to the ASA national convention in Orlando, Floirida in 1975 and the ASA commissioners dubbed them that name. Although they were unsuccessful that year with their bid, they were impressive enough to succeed the following year. 69 of the 101 commissioners voted yes in San Diego, California on the first ballot.

They quickly adopted that name "Red Coats". Members: Lee Ballard, Clyde Dexter, Lee Goulet, Don Kasper, Tom McCardle, Marty McGuire, Don Moffatt, John Pattison, Doyle Rowland, Marv Stein, Dan Stevens, Jimmy Walsh, Bill Welch, Jimmy Wright, Bill Humphrey, Jerry Hoffman, Dick Page and John Mahar.

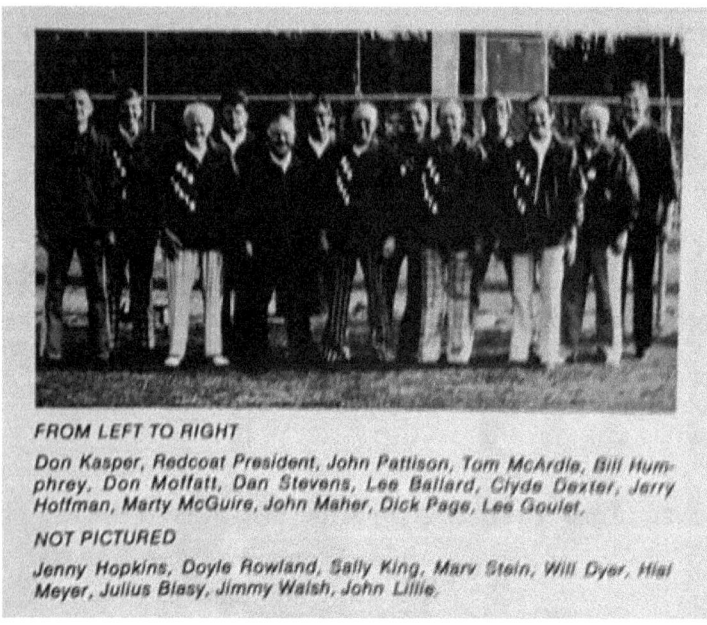

FROM LEFT TO RIGHT
Don Kasper, Redcoat President, John Pattison, Tom McArdle, Bill Humphrey, Don Moffatt, Dan Stevens, Lee Ballard, Clyde Dexter, Jerry Hoffman, Marty McGuire, John Maher, Dick Page, Lee Goulet.

NOT PICTURED
Jenny Hopkins, Doyle Rowland, Sally King, Marv Stein, Will Dyer, Hisl Meyer, Julius Blasy, Jimmy Walsh, John Lillie.

Photo of Red Coats members

Midland became the only community under 100,000 population to host such a large prestigious tournament. The actual population of the city was just over 38,000. The Midland Dow AC's helped put Midland on the national spotlight back in the early 50's with their outstanding team.

This time Midland would be represented by their host team,

McCardle Pontiac Cadillac. Defending champion Raybestos Cardinals out of Stratford, Connecticut and last year's runner-up Aurora Home Savings from Aurora, Illinois will be hoping to break their streak of three straight runner-up finishes. There would be a total of twenty teams entered in the tournament. Umpire-In-chief Tom Mason selected Bill Humphrey, was the deputy UIC. Jerry Hanson and Pete marsh from Midland were selected for the umpire crew along with ten others from around the country.

The largest crowd to ever attend a softball game in Midland, occurred on Wednesday evening, September 15, when McArdle's played Aurora in an undefeated matchup.

"I would guess there was 2,400 cars parked in Emerson Park," tournament director Don Moffatt said. "I heard of people walking almost a mile to get to the stadium."

The huge crowd tried to cheer the home team to victory but Aurora was just too strong and won by a 6-1 score. McArdle's would finish with an impressive 3-2 record and a 6th place finish. Four players would be named to the All-American team, Bruce Miller and Jeff Peck to the 1st team and pitcher Bob Ryan and Jim Fillion to the 2nd team.

"He wanted to pick my brain as to the best way to rate umpires for the rest of the tournament."

"I suggested the 'A-B-C' way, with A being the best." We then went through the umpires we had and rated them. Six were cut after their three games were completed.

Heavy rain played a huge part in the tournament as Tuesday games were postponed along with Thursday night games early in the tournament. Luckily the rain held off after the final pitch the championship game Saturday night to allow the midnight presentation of trophies.

"Aurora beat the undefeated Reading, Pennsylvania team 3-0 in the championship game to force an "IF" game. However, Reading proved to be too much for Aurora in that game as they were shutout 4-0 to finish in second place for the 4th straight year."

The day after the tournament ended, I picked up recreation director, Marty McGuire and drove us behind the stadium. I told Marty to look at all of the trash in the stadium and outside of it. He was shocked, especially when I followed up with, "I'm going to go after the '79 national tournament."

Prior to 1977, Bill had no staff as he was the state UIC. This changed quickly as Jack Sauder, Harry Fretenboro from Flint, Jim Wofford, and Paul Pironack were added. After being turned down the two previous years to have district UIC's, it was finally approved in 1977. Twenty UIC's and commissioners were selected.

Bill decided the first item needed was more training for the umpire program. The next item was the need to fulfill the uniforms needed by the umpires. When asked how this training would be paid for, Bill quickly responded be adding $4 dollars to the registration fee. He was told they wouldn't pay it and Bill quickly added again, "In a New York minute."

Once the executive board decided they wouldn't win this argument they approved the extra fee. Jack Sauder was assigned to visit the respective districts and the new state clinics and sell uniforms. He purchased $6,000 worth of uniforms out of his own pocked, packed his van full and quickly sold out. He bought another $6,000 worth of uniforms and sold them all too. This proved how determined and dedicated our umpires were.

The word was quickly spreading to the national office of how well the umpire program was progressing in Michigan under Bill's leadership. He was requested to speak at the 1978 UIC Clinic in Oklahoma City about plate mechanics. It didn't start off good,

"As I stepped onto the platform that was built, the corner broke off," Bill laughed about. "It didn't prevent me from speaking after the laughter stopped."

Humphrey was selected to umpire the Women's Class A Slow Pitch Tournament in Hamilton, Ohio., in 1978.

"I didn't know one umpire but I heard of Bernie Perfallow," Bill said. "While he was putting on his plate gear I observed something blue-grey on his ankle. I moved down to get a closer look and sure enough it was a pistol."

"Expecting trouble?" Bill quickly asked as he pointed to the gun.

"Oh Shit", Bernie suddenly said. (He was a police officer)

Tom Mason asked Bill to join the national umpire staff and he was surprised. "I didn't even know we had a national umpire staff," Bill laughed as he stated that. There was no umpire manual and no real organization in place. This would quickly change once Bill became the national deputy umpire-in-chief after ASA president Andy Pendergrass appointed him. When training began, registrations almost doubled and this continued for about 10-12 years. Again, **"Time and Place"**.

Bill was also selected to umpire softball at the National Sports Festival in Colorado Springs along with Jerry Hanson from Michigan. This was held from July 28-30 in 1978. This was sponsored by the U.S. Olympic Committee for 2,100 Olympic athletes.

Besides softball, twenty-three other sports were selected. Some of the other major sports were baseball, figure skating, gymnastics, ice hockey, swimming and track and field.

Humphrey recalled how touched he was by the opening ceremonies and of course the national anthem. "Tears were flowing down my cheeks," he said. "I will never forget that moment."

"One day we were rained out so a bunch of us umpires piled into a large Ford Wagoneer and headed out and just hung out," Bill recalled. "There is nothing to replace camaraderie at a tournament."

The Colorado Springs Sports page featured a comment by Bill Humphrey on the front page. Bill was talking to a group at Memorial Park on Sunday, July 30, Tom Mason, the ASA umpire-in-chief and Humphrey's boss walked in.

"You've heard of an umpire who thinks he's God," Bill asked. "Well, here's God and he thinks he's an umpire."

Ty Stofflet, pitcher for the Billard Barbell team from Reading, Pennsylvania team, proved to be too much as he struck out twelve Guanella Santa Rosa, California team members in a 3-0 shutout. Over 2,000 fans watched this performance in the championship game.

"The difference between him and other pitchers, is that you don't feel bad when you strike out against him," Dallas Roundtree of the Guanella team stated. "He's just the best there is," Roundtree added, "You don't know what to look for, he's so damn deceptive. You just go up there and hope to get the pitch your looking for."

This idea worked for Roundtree as he broke up Stofflet's no hit bid with one out in the seventh inning with a base hit.

On the women's side, the Sun City Saints upset the Raybestos Brakettes from Stafford, Connecticut 1-0, in the championship game. Paula Noel tossed a one hitter, facing just twenty-two batters and driving in the only run of the game. Losing pitcher, Barbara Reinalda, broke up the no hitter in the fifth inning with a bloop single to right field. Like Stofflet, losing the no hitter meant little to Noel, compared to the excitement of having a gold medal hanging from your neck.

"We train umpire for national tournaments. There's difference in training and doing. We never did this before. If the umpires don't want to do put in the effort, you are wasting your time"

Midland once again hosted the men's major national tournament in 1979 after winning the bid. It would be held from September 7-15. Again, the Midland Redcoats were instrumental in acquiring this prestigious tournament. Bill Humphrey was the president of the Midland Redcoats and wrote a letter which appeared in the official program.

"We, the redcoats, along with the City Council, Midland softball association and the department of Parks and Recreation take great pride in presenting to you the 1979 ASAP men's national fastpitch tournament.

We would like to thank the 1978 ASA commissioner's council for granting us the permission to host this year's national tournament and extend their gratitude to all the people and organizations in our community who have made this event possible.

Once again the Dow, Gerstacker and Strosacker foundations, have answered our call for additional site improvements. The acquisition of the outfield bleachers with the seating capacity of 2000 seats is a direct result of their support and should prove beneficial for many years to come with numerous recreational endeavors.

In 1977, you could hear the call ring out, 'the redcoats are coming, the redcoats are coming.' Now in 1979, you can hear the call, 'the red coats are back, the red coats are back,' and with this call, we would like to dedicate this to you, the fan because you are responsible for making the great game of softball what it is today.

Enjoy yourself and have a pleasant stay in our community."

Sincerely,

Bill Humphrey

This national tournament would put Midland on the map in many ways. In 1977, Midland set the record for attendance when over 75,000 enthusiastic fans watched the games. The 1979 national tournament would smash that record as nearly 90,000 spectators attended. Very notable for a city under 40,000 population. Twelve umpires from around the country were selected with Pete Marsh and Jerry Hanson selected from Midland.

The most notable achievement would happen when the tournament championship game ended. But that's getting ahead of the story. McCardle needed nine innings to break a scoreless tie in the Loser Bracket Final. Coach Terry Collins decided to play "small ball" in the ninth advancing Bob Servoss who came in to run for Evans Telegadas at first base after he singled and move to second after a walk to Rod Johnson. Nels Conkright laid down a perfect sacrifice bunt to advance Servoss to third and Johnson to second. Then came "the play" on a perfect suicide squeeze bunt by first baseman, Lee Wright, to score pinch runner, Bob Servoss from third on a close play at home.

Photo of Servoss scoring

8,911 fans, mostly home towners, watched Owen "The Fog" Walford from McArdle's and Roy Burleson from O'Byrne Electric from Springfield, Missouri, put on a marvelous pitching performance. As the fans roared, Midland's bench emptied knowing they achieved the opportunity to play in the finals of the winner's bracket. This will not be an easy task as they will face last year's defending champions, Bob Hoffman's York Barbell team from Reading, Pennsylvania, who won earlier, 3-1 in eight innings against Southern Truck Raiders from Phoenix. A win in that game would propel McArdle's into the championship game on Saturday night.

The great Ty Stofflett and his streak of winning 14 consecutive games in ASA championship play would be no easy task. It would take ten innings and superb pitching by Wolford to escape with a 1-0 win despite nineteen strikeouts by Stofflett. Now the stage was set for the "winner take all" championship game.

McArdle's would send out Bob Ryan to face York's Larry Berg. Jeff Peck would play the key roll in all three rallies by McArdle's and claim the MVP award. Amazingly enough, McArdle's, the host team would fight their way through the loser bracket and claim the ASA national title with a 3-1 win.

Peck's .455 average, 10 for 22 and 2 RBI's allowed him to win the MVP award and Ty Stofflett won the Most Outstanding Pitcher Award going 5-1, 46 innings pitched, 76 strikeouts and 2 one-hit shutouts. Walford, Peck, Cronkright, Ryan, and Jack Starling would be named to the First Team All American squad. Evan Telegades would be selected to the Second All American Team.

The 70's would introduce the aluminum bat to softball. The first bat was manufactured for use in 1968 by the Amerola Products, a Pittsburgh manufacturer of aluminum pool cues. Using an aluminum tube and a wooden handle they fashioned the bat by using metal rivets to hold the rubber insert in place on the end of the bat.

Owner Tony Merola had his bat tested for use by ASA under the trademark, "Trucue". The bat was approved by ASA at their January 1969 convention. Legal status was now obtained. The era of the aluminum bat had begun and numerous bat manufacturers were rushing to get a foothold in this market.

Worth pounced first. In 1970 they produced a stronger aluminum alloy with a 2.25 inch diameter, more suitable for softball. They also used a rolled lip on the end to hold the end plug in place rather than metal rivets. Plus the bat's molded grip contained a molded knob, which replaced the wooden knob.

Most slow pitch players preferred a heavier bat, up to 40 ounces. The Bombat brand became a very popular bat because of the heavier bats they produced. ASA concluded that heavier bats might increase distance, set a 38 ounce weight limit, a standard that still remains in the rule book. Today a 30 ounce bat is considered heavy.

It would be twenty more years before modern day performance testing would put better standards in place. Amerol products would cease manufacturing bats by the mid-70's. All bat manufacturers were now hustling to be the best for the market share.

HOF Sculpture unveiled

The decade ended with the unveiling of the "Play at Home" sculpture dedicated on June 23, 1979 at the Hall of Fame. The popular sculpture by Leonard McMurray quickly became a favorite for players and fans alike.

Photo of sculpture

"We can teach you when to get there, how to get there, and what to do but you have to have game presence. How do you react to game situations? How do you put that into words? You have to be a student of the game and know the rules."

Bill Humphrey

Chapter Ten

Softball Celebrates 100 Years

The decade of the 80's was a milestone one. Strangely it was the Major League Baseball strike in 1981 which opened the door for ASA to televise softball. The players strike caused a 713 game cancellation and the fans were clamoring for a game to watch.

ESPN was looking for avenues to show sporting events and softball seemed like a perfect fit. ASA was contacted and on June 1981, showcased it first formal Hall of fame induction ceremony. Four events were featured and named the Hall of Fame Classic.

The Oklahoma City Jets girls fast pitch team versus China was the feature along with a national home run hitting contest. A slow pitch game between national champions Rubi-Otts from Graham, North Carolina and Women's Major All-Americans was played followed by induction of Hall of Famers; Harvey Sterkel, Carol Spanks, Shirley Topley, George Adam and Bill Parker, all fast pitch standouts.

MLB greats Lou Brock and Oklahoma great, Mickey Mantle were special guests and this certainly helped publicize the ceremonies. ESPN filmed all four events and televised them via replay in July. The games were played at Eggeling stadium at Wheeling Park in Oklahoma City. The 3,378 fans attending the fast pitch game was a record at that time for a softball game in Oklahoma City.

The ASA Junior Olympic program reached record numbers in

1982 with over 22,000 teams and more than 440,000 participants. Two major sponsors agreed to pay for the major portions of the sport. Wilson Sporting Goods from Chicago footed the 1983 program and Coca-Cola agreed to sponsor the awards for the regional and national tournaments.

The 80's could also be called the "moving decade" for Bill Humphrey.

Now that he was settled into his role on the national umpire staff, he would be more outspoken, perhaps more demanding on what he thought was needed. Bill was gaining more respect whenever he spoke because he would back up his statements with fact!

NATIONAL UMPIRE STAFF: Members include front row (from left) Rex Brown, Region 15; Max Wilkes, Region 5; Johnny Welton, Region 14; Walt Sparks, Region 7; and Dave Epperson, Region 12. Middle row (from left) Bill Humphrey, Region 8; Bill Peterson, Region 11; Ed Dressler, Region 2; Len Friedlund, Region 13; Dan Blair, Region 4; and Merle Burler, ASA National Director of Umpires. Back row (from left) Bernie Profato, Region 9; Henry Pollard, Region 3; Horace Bruff, Region 6; Al Cenci, Region 1; and Ron Jeffers, Region 10. (Photo by Claude Long)

Photo of national umpire staff (1981)

Because Bill was now on the national umpire staff, he would not be selected as an umpire for any national tournaments with ASA. However, this would provide him many opportunities to be a UIC for those tournaments.

Bill bowed out of the 1980 Men's major world championship tournament in Tacoma, Washington. There was an "unwritten rule" that you couldn't have two umpires from the same state. This set his retirement back about four years as he wanted to umpire one more big tournament.

"There were two umpires selected from Midland, myself and Jerry Hanson. The tournament UIC didn't want that and neither did Don Porter, so I bowed out." Bill stated.

Jack Sauder would take over as the state UIC for Michigan and his staff would comprise of Paul Pioronak, Jim Wolford, Harry Frattenboro from Flint, and Ron Sorrell. S hortly thereafter, Ron Welch took over for Ron Sorrell. Sauder put a new direction in place due to the influence of Humphrey.

"We had manuals for everything. Wolford put the program in writing. We had printed guidelines for tournament directors and UIC's, along with guidelines for district UIC's." Bill added, "When a tournament director came into the office he was handed printed up documents in folders for use."

As we sat in Tim Tony's restaurant in Saginaw, Bill followed up with a story about a road trip he and Jack took in Michigan.

"I was the state UIC and Jack was basically my right hand man. Nobody did more with so little than Jack. Absolutely dedicated to softball!"

"We left Bay City on the way to Caseville in the thumb. They played a slow pitch tournament on Saturdays and a modified tournament on Sundays. It was an ideal situation for recruiting." Bill smiled as he talked about how it went. "We watched umpires, we talked to them, we talked to the teams. When it was over, we had over 50 teams registered to play with MASA and close to 20 umpires registered."

"You can't run a softball organization from the office."

Jack added, "The one thing I learned from Bill was when we started a program, it was like building a house. You start with a good foundation and work your way up. Later on, if you need a door, build it."

Then Bill told a story about going to Edmore, Michigan. "We immediately thought about the great pitcher, Edmore Johnson. We laughed as we said they had to name this town after him." Bill added, "He always wanted a new ball and an old one to look at before he pitched. Of course he wanted the old one….that didn't work."

Jack jumped in, "I believe he played for a team called 'Dave's Sanitation.' I had him in a game where he walked past second base into center field and sat down. Then he yelled out he wanted some grapes. Yes, grapes. It turns out he was on parole and he loved grapes when he was incarcerated. His parole officer attended just about every one of his games."

The March/April 1980 edition of "Balls & Strikes" mentioned the election of Marty McGuire as the new president of MASA, replacing Val Millholland. McGuire was the director of the Midland recreation department at the time.

Bill would be appointed the UIC for the 1981 ASA Men's National Fast Pitch tournament in St. Joseph, Missouri. The main park would be Phil J. Welch stadium and the dates were September 11 – 19. Two teams from Michigan were entered out of the 24 team field. The Bolters from Saginaw and Plangger's Furniture from Benton Harbor.

Twelve umpires from many states were selected. Jack Sauder and Henry Flowers would represent Michigan. "We drove out in a van with no seats in the back," Bill said as he laughed. "We put lawn chairs in the back to sit on."

Ashland beat ADM with a 2-0 victory behind the shutout pitching of Hank Miller and forcing the extra game. ADM's Mike Fenton hit an 11th inning single scoring Brian Rothrock with the winning run to win the championship.

"You cannot legislate good umpiring. It takes talent and teaching."

The decade of the 80's would see two of the greatest fast pitch teams in the nation face each other numerous times. Less than 20 miles apart, The Bolters from Saginaw, Michigan and Midland Valley Mechanical Contracting or Midland McArdles (same team, different sponsor) would face each other over twenty times.

If played in Saginaw it would usually be Hoyt Park and if in Midland, it would be at Currie stadium. Hoyt Park would witness hundreds of people sitting on the hill to watch the games. Bill Humphrey, Jack Sauder, George Becker, and other great umpires would be assigned to these "league games".

The ISC World Tournament would be held at Veteran's stadium in Saginaw, Michigan in August of 1981 and it would feature the longest softball game in championship play when Midland VMC would outlast The Farm, from Madison, Wisconsin in 34 innings. The game began in the early evening on Tuesday, August 18 and ended at 1:30 am the next day, thanks to a game winning single by Dave "Tuck" Bedford.

Pitchers Peter Finn from Midland VMC and Peter Meredith from the Farm went the distance. Finn would fan 64 batters to break the record by twenty strikeouts. Amazingly enough, the next day a 28 inning game was played between Tulsa and Ashland tying the record for the second longest game ever.

"I was fortunate to live in an area that had the best to offer, in regards to softball."

Bill also umpired the College World Series in 1981 and recalled a call he had in a game between Indiana and South Carolina. "Girl was probably safe by a full step and I called her out. Coach came out to argue and I remained in the set position. His gum started to come out of his mouth and he had to shove it back in. I started to laugh and he did too and that was the end of the discussion."

The men's national fastpitch tournament would be held in Midland and Humphrey would be the UIC again. The Redcoats would be instrumental once again, in obtaining the tournament.

There were twelve umpires selected with Jerry Hanson and George Mallory representing Michigan, and both being from Midland. Bob Kelly from Saginaw would be the umpire coordinator.

The Saginaw Bolters with Kevin Herlihy pitching and the Midland Explorers with Peter Finn would represent Michigan in the twenty-six team field. ADM from Decatur, Illinois would return to defend their title.

ADM from Decatur, Illinois beat Peterbuilt Western from Seattle in the championship game 6 to 4 which forced the "IF" game. Peterbilt pitcher Jimmy Moore hurled a 2 hit shutout to clinch the title for the Seattle team. Larry Seabaugh's base hit scored Kim Sullivan with the first run in the fifth inning. Sullivan later scored on Greg vanGavers sacrifice fly in the 7th inning to account for all the scoring.

The legendary Jimmy Doyle of the Ashland Merchants tossed all 32 innings for his team at the age of 48, going 2-2. The Explorers would finish in 5th place with a 5-2 record while the Bolters would tie for 13th place with a 2-2 record despite Herlihy tossing a no-hitter for the Bolters.

There was numerous rule changes during the 80's, and Bill, being on the national umpire staff, was instrumental in either getting them adopted, amended or dismissed. He would stand up, and in either a short or long dialog, explain the reasoning behind it. When Bill spoke, people listened, because his reasoning involved facts not just talk. One time there was talk of putting in the "tie breaker" for fast pitch. Bill quickly convinced the board this was a bad idea.

Bill explained, "From time to time we would come up with rules that would restrict pitching. I was the one who went to the fast pitch rules committee and I said, lets get rid of the BS! First, we need to enforce the rule as written then we can change it. One foot on the rubber, let's pitch. Forward step. Don't pass rules you can't enforce. Do not knit pick! We have language for the crow hop and the leap. Enforce it!"

Tom Mason, Chief Clinician and National Rule wrote in the April, 1983 issue of "Balls & Strikes". "Umpires were instructed to enforce the pitching rule beginning with the first day of the season. Be aware of pitching rule violations but don't haunt the pitcher. Remember also that we should not enforce the rule in degrees. The pitcher is either on the pitcher's plate or he isn't; he is either outside the 24" length of the pitcher's plate or he isn't; he either crow hops or he doesn't. There is no such thing as 'He violated the rule only a little'."

Umpires wore a powder blue Elbeco shirt. When the military press was used and it was fresh, it looked good. However, it was uncomfortable. Bill wanted different colors. He liked the dark blue but it didn't look good on the navy blue pants, which was the only pants allowed at the time. Bill like the idea of a white shirt. It wasn't until 20 plus years later that many shirt colors were adopted. Bill never gave up on this idea and his persistence finally won out. Even a pink shirt can now be used for umpiring!

"I always wanted a cotton pull over shirt and I always wanted more than one color."

Although the powder blue Elbeco shirt was the only shirt allowed for tournament play, the cotton shirt was allowed for local associations, per approval of the local area commissioner and association officers.

Walt Balcom, MASA Executive Secretary, wrote this in his article "Michigan Amateur Softball History", which appeared in the 1982 MASA Softball Championship program.

"The history of MASA would not be complete without a word of praise for the advancement of the Michigan softball umpire program. National deputy umpire-in-chief William Humphrey and state umpire-in chief Jack Sauder and his staff have built our statewide program into probably the best umpires organization in the Amateur Softball Association. The senior umpire staff comprised of Jerry Hanson, Harry Fretenborough, Bob Glowacki and Ron Welch, conduct all day umpire clinics in each of the 18 MASA districts as well as many personal clinics of their own. MASA trained umpires are much sought after to work Michigan high school girls interscholastic schedules."

"1984 would be the last year of umpiring for me. I didn't get a chance to achieve all of the goals I set for myself."

1985

A record 293 umpires from the United States attended the 9th biannual National Rules Seminar and UIC Clinic in Oklahoma City on February 15-17, 1985. It was deemed the "best ever held".

Six umpires were selected for ISF certification with Jack Sauder being one of them in the fast pitch category. He would be be chosen with others for the Junior World Fast Pitch Championship to be held in Fargo, North Dakota. This prestigious tournament is only held every four years.

ASA COMMITTED: Red Halpern (left), chairman of the ASA Special Programs/Special Olympics Committee, shakes hands with Bob Rodwell, director of softball for Special Olympics, to pledge ASA's support of Special Olympics. At right is ASA President Charles L. McCord. (Photo by James Coleman)

Photo of handshake

Softball and ASA took a step closer to becoming a sport for just about everyone when the Special Olympics and ASA agreed to join together for the betterment of the sport.

Red Helpern, chairman of the ASA Special Programs/Special Olympics committee, stated, "our goal, down the road, is to be able to Co sponsor with Special Olympics state softball tournaments in every state."

Softball has become a $20 million industry in Michigan and could reach $50 million if expenditures from local leagues were added in. Michigan officials project that more than 750,000 individuals will play in various leagues throughout the state this summer and that almost 236,800 will participate in one of the 740 tournaments set for 1985.

Ten national umpire schools were conducted in the United States in 1985. Each school is limited to just 75 participants, due mostly to over 65,000 umpires registered. Bill Humphrey was a key factor in the "birth" of national umpire schools.

1986

The USA team captured the Women's World's Fast Pitch Championship in Aukland, New Zealand on January 17-28. The team was unbeaten (13-0) and beat heavily favored China for the trophy.

"Everyone kept telling us we had to watch out for China, we had to watch out for New Zealand, we had to watch out for Canada," said Ralph Raymond the coach of the defending national USA champions. "I kept telling the kids, these other countries had to watch out for us. We had a mission, and that was to win the world championship."

What was truly amazing is a 16 year old high school phenom was the star pitcher for the women. Michele Granger, a left hander from Placentia, California won two games (one perfect game) and saved another against Canada working out of a no-out bases loaded jam in the top of the 7th inning with two key strikeouts and a fly ball out. In the game against favored New Zealand, she came within an out of another perfect game.

Photo of Michele Granger

Metro Detroit received an award for the largest increase (24%) in registered teams. Bill Svochak, Detroit commissioner also received a service award for 15 years. Matt Urban, MASA commissioner received a 25 year service award. Mack Phillips, from Grosse Pointe was named to the Hall of Fame in the meritorious Service category. He became the second person from Michigan to receive that honor.

Midland would once again host a fast pitch tournament. This time the women would be showcased during the ASA Class A national and the total attendance would top 20,000 for the week long event.

1987

Centennial Poster

ASA unveiled the "Centennial" poster to commemorate 100 years of softball. The Amateur Softball Association began in 1937. A 800 "torch run" will take place this summer, beginning in Chicago, where the Great game of softball was invented on June 29 and end in Oklahoma City, home of ASA national headquarters on July 10. There would be numerous events and festivities during the course of the year to celebrate this tremendous accomplishment.

A special memorial monument will be unveiled on the site where the Faragat Boat Club was located, now the Michael Reese Medical Center and Hospital on Lake Shore Drive.

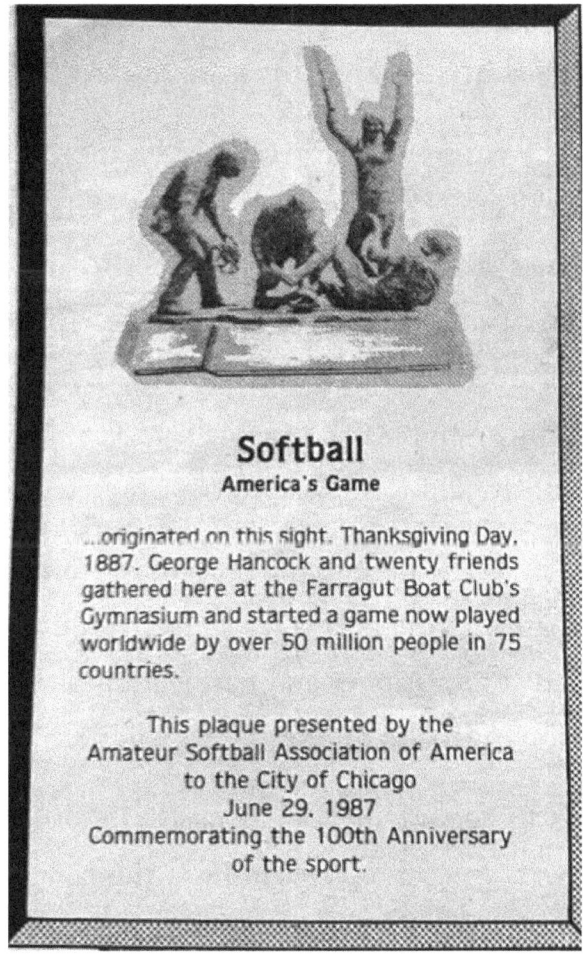

Memorial Monument

How fitting that in the 100th year, Bill Humphrey would become the 15th umpire enshrined in the ASA National Hall of Fame. He would be joined by Henry Flowers of Copely, Ohio.

"I wasn't sure if I was to be considered for induction into the Hall of Fame because I didn't meet the requirements of umpiring in three major tournaments and I felt that my induction would hurt the program.

I was assured me that there was other criteria that I met, such as the Pan Am Games and Sports Festival softball that I umpired."

Five umpires were selected for ISF certification, all in the fast pitch category. Penny Knupp from Lansing, Michigan was one of the five, once again showing the excellence in umpiring in Michigan. The National Indicator Fraternity (NIF) in its first year, approved 168 members. Gary Evans, Jerry Hanson, Bill Humphrey, Penny Knupp, George Mallery, Pete Marsh, Richard Ribby, Jack Sauder, and Ron Welch would represent Michigan.

To qualify for NIF, an umpire must have umpired in three national tournaments and been a registered ASA umpire for seven years. The local commissioner and national umpire staff member from that region must also approve the application.

Pennsylvania let the way in seat purchases ($100 or $200 each) with 29 box seats and 56 reserved seats at the new ASA stadium. Michigan was second with 39 box seats bought. A total of $45,250 was raised with this program.

On October 3, a time capsule commemorating the 100th year of the sport of softball was buried in front of the new ASA Hall of Fame stadium in Oklahoma City. It was filled with rule books, uniforms, bats, balls and .other memorabilia from the game of softball.

1988

The USA team was too much for China and Japan as they won the third Tri-Nation Women's Championship at the ASA Hall of Fame stadium. The event took place from July 8-10. Michele Granger, now 18, beat China three times, all shutouts, 1-0, 3-0, and 2-0. Debbie Doom beat Japan twice, 10-0 and 1-0. Suzie Gaw and Liz Mizera were the star hitters collecting 36 hits in 117 at bats.

ASA announced that an advanced school for umpires would be offered in 1989. It will be available only for those umpires who attended previous national umpire schools. Once again, there will be ten national schools offered this year for umpires. Bill was very instrumental in the idea of an advanced school, once again showing his perspective in what was needed for the umpire program.

The Hi-Ho Brakettes from Stratford, Connecticut won their 20th national championship, defeating reigning champions, Majestics, from California, 2-1. The Majestics lost their first game of the Women's Major tournament but battled back behind the great pitching of Michele Granger and 17 year old Lisa Fernandez. Gina Vecchione batted .444 (8 for 18) for the Brakettes.

1989

Bert Weeks, the president of ASA, announced there would be 50 national tournaments this year and any team that wants to play in one has the opportunity.

The first ever ASA Commissioners' Seminar was held in Oklahoma City from February 23-25. Of the 101 commissioners, 82 attended. The idea for the seminar was to advise commissioners on how to promote, organize, and sell the ASA to teams and umpires.

For the third time in the decade, Midland would host a men's fast pitch national tournament. The Redcoats worked diligently to host their 5th ASA fast pitch tournament in the 80's. After the '82 and '84 Men's World tournament, there was the Women's Class A in '86, the Women's Class B in '88, and now the Men's Major on September 8-16 in 1989. They also hosted the National Association of Intercollegiate Athletics Championships (NAIA) Women's Softball in the summer of 1989.

Bill Humphrey, a member of the Redcoats, was assigned housing for his responsibilities. Marty McGuire was the tournament director. Eleven other members along with president, Lee Goulet worked tirelessly to make the tournament a success.

The umpire-in-chief would once again be Bill Humphrey! He would be in charge of nineteen umpires with seven being from Michigan. They were: Jerry Hanson, Tom Hutfilz, George

Mallory, Dick Ribby, Jack Sauder, Bryan Smith (now umpire-in-chief of USA Softball of Michigan), and Kevin Ryan (now director of umpires for USA Softball). Craig Cress from Terre Haute, Indiana (now executive director of USA Softball) was also on the crew.

Chapter Eleven

Bill Humphrey Becomes President of ASA

"The main reason I ran for president was of the need to separate the ISF from ASA," Bill emphasized. "Don Porter was in charge of ASA and ISF and he was given carte blanc to start a world organization by the powers that be to get us into the Olympics."

Photo of Bill Humphrey

Later, the ISF was moved out of Oklahoma City to Florida. "I just needed seven more votes in order to win, but I didn't want a 'war'", Bill stated. "I wanted a letter of resignation. He no longer had the seven votes and I eventually did. When the votes were tabulated I became president."

"When I was director of membership, I showed them how they could save millions of dollars by simply not printing a rule book." Bill added, "I had many ideas that I wanted to accomplish. I needed the position to get those through."

"Getting the national umpire schools was big and it was because of Ron Jeffers and Tom Mason and myself, not just me. In 1979 that idea was turned down by the board of directors and it wasn't until much later that ASA decided those schools would benefit the umpire program. Pat Atkinson from Alabama finally convinced the council."

The first national school was held in Indianapolis and ninety umpires attended and afterwards their surveys said they were overwhelmingly in favor of more. It began with five schools, then expanded to seven or eight and then eventually in each region. Today there are numerous national schools offered throughout the country.

"Jerry Hanson and myself met at Ron Jeffers house in Cincinnati and discussed how we would dissect responsibilities for the first school. We broke for dinner and ate at a restaurant on the Ohio River to discuss more details. The next day we had breakfast and

Ron said he would do plate drills. Mason would do instruction and interference and he had 95% of the agenda complete. I would do mechanics because nobody knew that better, according to Tom."

"Some of our mechanics were really outdated. An umpire making a safe call looked like a bird pecking at food. Tom said we need a new manual on mechanics so I decided to do that myself," Bill added.

"The schools were extremely successful and ASA has trained thousands of umpires," Bill stated. "The board of directors were concerned that umpires wouldn't pay for the school. We charged $75 per umpire hoping to get 60. We got 90!"

When Bill's presidency ended, he never stopped being involved with ASA or MASA. He would continue advising umpires whenever he was a UIC of a tournament or just a spectator. "I probably was the UIC of over 30 tournaments," Bill added.

He would become the state commissioner of MASA and would make numerous changes for the benefit of the program. He would continue until 2000 when he would turn over the reins to Jerry Hanson.

"Everything changed when Bill took over," Debbie Sherwood said. "We entered the computer age in the office, and it wasn't an easy transformation for either of us. We worked through it and Bill worked on making MASA the best organization in ASA."

"Referee Magazine" selected Bill Humphrey as one of the fifty-two most influential in officiating history. Quite an accomplishment when one considers how many thousands, if not millions, of officials of sports there have been.

"At one time we had 30 umpires in Michigan who were ISF certified, which was unbelievable. For instance, Region 3 only had three. Michigan was far and above many states and regions when it came to umpiring," Bill stated. "We were already training our umpires and preparing them for national tournaments."

When Bill stepped away from the MASA state commissioner position, he stayed involved by being the ASA player representative at numerous fast pitch and modified national tournaments well into the 21st century. He was well respected by umpires and players alike.

It didn't matter if it was a local high school game, a college game or a recreation game during the season, many times Bill could be seen sitting behind the back stop watching umpires more than the game.

The "Midland Daily News" had an article on Bill the year he was presented the Merle Butler national award. "As they were talking I knew they were talking about me. I was certainly not expecting it. I don't do things for rewards. But it is nice to be recognized and appreciated," Bill said.

The article went on to state that Humphrey was especially proud of quality of umpires that he has produced at every level. He has demanded professionalism at all times and in every phase of the job. From conduct on the field to the apparel they wear. "It has been a lot of fun and keeps me involved. After all this time I still enjoy the game," Bill stated.

Bill has been inducted into six Hall of Fames! They are:

1982 – MASA Hall of Fame

1986 – IASA Hall of Fame (Indiana)

1987 – ASA National Hall of Fame

1992 – Midland County Sports Hall of Fame

1998 – Indianapolis Metro ASA Hall of Fame

2016 – Detroit Metro ASA Hall of Fame

Bill reflected on all of the great pitchers he faced in his career. The list is quite remarkable:"

He faced Bonnie Jones as a teenager at the plate as a hitter and later behind the plate as an umpire. "He had so many different pitches you never knew what was coming. He had what I call a high-drop ball. He would challenge the batters."

"Herlihy was the best by far. Never saw one better. He could hit a postage stamp if needed. I doubt if he ever threw a pitch down the middle."

"Darren Zach was 6'5" and weighed about 350. Man, could he bring it! Nobody threw faster than him. Pure intimidation!"

"Ty Stofflet holds records that will never be broken. Another pitcher who could hit spots. His first pitch was usually nothing but smoke. Wherever the catcher put the glove, that's where it went."

"Strickland was another one who could hit a pin cushion."

"Clyde Dexter I used to catch warming up when I was just a kid. He wanted to make a pitcher out of me. He was amazing."

"Bob Ryan was another great local pitcher but couldn't throw a good changeup. "

"Jimmy Doyle could throw all day and all night. He had a rubber arm. Another pitcher who couldn't throw a good changeup."

Other pitchers Bill named that he faced: Jerry Hoffman, Peter Finn, Lefty Ross, Ralph Minnis, Richard Plangger, Jack Greenwood, Lyn Ackerman, Rod Dewey, George Luther, Ernie Sirrine, Guy Manke, Don Hingston, Kathy Arendsen, Jim Volk, Gene Engle, Tom Beale, George Wheelock, Russell Ackerman, Ken Bosch, Newton Mapes, Larry Rousseau, Ken Richardson, James Roekle, Jim Trier, Al Gloden, Gary Dresch, Al Hector, Leo Urban, Tom Paul, Greg Wright, and Dave Dufon.

Bill was asked to name his five favorite ball parks or fields to umpire on. He quickly said Currie Stadium, Petoskey, Ranney Park in Lansing, Pine Grove in Port Huron and Scottsville, which was just 15 miles east of Ludington.

Bill would mention umpires from time to time when we talked.

"Dave Selden is just the best in the world! He can handle any style of pitching and just does it smoothly. If he has a bad game its still good."

"Rick Havercroft is another umpire that if he has a bad game its still a good one. Nobody better behind the plate. Doesn't get rattled."

"Paul Piornack, by far the best slow pitch umpire I ever saw. Just put him out there and watch him."

"Jack Sauder could umpire any game because of his demeanor. If it got too heated, nobody could settle down a game better than him."

"The Evans brothers, Gary and Jamie. Just as smooth as glass and nothing but hustle."

"George Mallory and myself umpired many games together. I knew where he would always be."

"Bryan Smith, of course I'm not a fan of his wide plate stance but he manages to get out of it and down the line. He's done a lot of big games."

"Dick Ribby had a different style than most umpires but he sure was great. I loved having him on a crew."

"I'm sure Bill could have made a comment about just about any umpire, but I never brought names up." Dave Schimpf says. "It was better to just let Bill talk and write it down."

Ron Welch said this at a lunch with Bill and I. "I was called a women's fast pitch umpire because I umped women in Bay City and then the women's major fast pitch tournament. I also umpired modified because that got me to a national tournament."

Bill chimed in, "I was trying to get you to the Olympics. Havercroft was ISF certified in modified before he ever got certified in men's fast pitch. He did so well that he was requested back every time."

Umpire-in-Chiefs

When asked about the many UIC's over the years on the state staff, Bill was quite candid. He would compare most to his philosophy.

"Our state staff had many different ideas and personalities, but when the day ended, ASA came out first," Bill stated. "I know I was a little tough at times but if you don't demand it you won't get it."

"Jack Sauder took over for me when I went on the national staff. He would tackle any job and get it done. We never missed a beat when he took over."

"Jim Wolford was a lot like me. Tough and demanding. He had

a red pencil that he used to emphasize a point. He got a lot done whenever it was asked of him."

"Ted Germain was also a lot like me but he had an easy demeanor unlike me," Bill laughed as he said that. "He only asked for excellence and to use our mechanics. He got the message through his way."

"Gary Evans was more laid back than me but he did require our umpires to be the best. He did want excellence from our umpires."

"Bryan Smith and Jerry Hanson both had different personalities from me. Same philosophy, just a different way of presenting."

"Jim Craig for instance has an easy going demeanor but he's tough! You don't replace a Jim Craig or a Julie Johnson. "

"What a clinician Julie Johnson was. The NCAA wanted Julie to work for them for a salary. She turned them down to work for ASA. Now that's dedication!"

"As a tournament UIC, you do a little pre-planning when it came to assignments. However, I never made final selections before evaluating umpires," Bill emphasized. "I had a 9 day national tournament played on one field. That was easy to see every umpire."

Bill added, "I had a UIC at a national tournament who had the entire umpire schedule made out! How do you know who can handle situations and perform in a tough game."

"I only had one tournament where I didn't have the plate for the championship game, Bill said. "It was in 1984, my last tournament, and Nick Cinquanto was on the plate and I was at 1st. It was the right decision.

At the men's major fast pitch in North Mankato, Minnesota in 1991 Jack got the plate assignment for the final game. The UIC drew straws with three umpires and Jack got the short one," Bill laughed."

"How do you take personalities out of an evaluation? How do you remove yourself from personal impressions when evaluating? Take that first impression and put it in its place," Bill added. "Selden and Ribby have two totally different styles. What makes them who they are is how they handle situations."

Quotes

There were many quotes by umpires who would be with Bill and myself as we talked. I thought about interjecting them throughout the book, but then thought it better to add them in the last chapter.

Ron Costello told this golf story: "One of the guys we were playing with got mad and threw a golf club into the Tittabawassee River. Bill instantly threw his putter in the river and said, 'Now that's a throw!' Later the joke was, When you talk about the river, that's where Bill keeps his golf clubs."

Bill had this umpire story, "I told a batter after he struck out on a change up. You missed your chance Hot Dog, because you will never see that pitch again."

"I was the one who put the stop to the four umpire system in tournaments. Jack told Henry Pollard to put four Michigan umpires on a game. There is too much thinking needed for an umpire in a four man system. We teach three man for a reason, just use that," Bill said.

Jack Sauder told a story about Gene McWilly, a pitcher from Canada. "He would warm up with a 16" ball on the sidelines then take a 12" ball and throw from 2nd base warming up. It sounded like a bomb but looked like a baseball when it hit the catcher's mitt."

Ron Welch: "I never knew what 'Old Style' was until I umpired a national in Green Bay, Wisconsin. I got introduced to Old Style Beer there."

Bill told this story: "Rod Peterson was another pitcher who warmed up with a 16" ball. A batter bailed out on a tight pitch and I heard a 'tick'. As he goes to first I follow him and then the coach came out."

He says to me, "Did you see that ball hit him?"

I replied, "Did you? I have a philosophy. The ball doesn't belong in the batter's box!"

He turned around and walked away. To this day Bill says the ball doesn't belong in the batter's box.

Jack Sauder told this one. "We had a good ole boy from Alabama who called an illegal pitch. He said in the locker room that he did that because it was what Bill wanted. Bill told him, I don't want controversy, I want to see how controversy is handled! The next Day I had a meeting to discuss the pitching rule again.

Jeff Yorke said it best about Bill, "You were very demanding, but you made it fun."

Another story by Bill: "Joe Squires sent Larry Fisher over to talk to me after he was asked where I was. Joe said he's sitting in the 2nd row behind the backstop where he always is. We talked for six hours about fast pitch and ISC versus ASA."

Bill again, "We had softball in the Olympics from 1996 to 2008. The host team many times has a major say in what sports are played. When we joined forces with baseball, it was one of the dumbest things we ever did. The MLB gave 250 thousand to get more women into the game."

"We should have got involved in the pro softball league when it started," Bill said. "Get about six teams, 60 players, and with $240,000 we could have run it."

Chris Armijo said this about restrictions on players. "If you played in Wyoming (Michigan) you couldn't play in Grand Rapids, and vice versa."

More from Bill

"I umpired for 25 years and never got hit in the throat or the jewels. Then one game a class D pitcher who threw hard, I got one under the throat protector. Two innings later I took a cup shot. I take the ball to the pitcher and he's kind of laughing. I said there is nothing wrong with this ball but the ones down below hurt pretty bad."

"Tom Gilstead was having trouble remembering the count behind the plate one time. He asked me for the count and I yelled back, Why the hell aren't you paying attention."

"During a men's fast pitch tournament in Ludington in 1972 we had a play where the 2nd baseman used a fake tag which at that time wasn't an obstruction rule just an unsportsmanlike rule. I made that change happen."

"Paul Piornack got a good rating at a tournament and I asked the UIC why, because there was no explanation. He changed that to an excellent afterwards."

"The MLB had some batter reaction statistics from about 1968, that showed a batter had from .13 -.28 seconds to decide to swing or not. They will lose sight of the ball from about six feet in front of the plate. When we moved the pitcher's rubber back to 43 feet I talked to Kathy Ahrenson, one of the top pitchers, about what affect that would have.

I said the movement would improve, drop ball, rise balls, curve balls would now also dominate. I was proved to be correct."

"When we wrote the umpire manual, Don Porter turned it over to some lawyers in D.C. to see if there could be a potential lawsuit. When told what they said, I said, What the hell is he for? He isn't going to tell me what uniform or shoes to wear!"

Finally, what could be more fitting to finish this book on Bill Humphrey than what he told me back in October of 2021. Now, don't take this wrong, Bill is still with us, but this is what he is all about and I know he said this for a reason.

"My funeral service after I'm cremated will have the song Take Me Out To The Ballgame and then everyone will call out, Strike One, Strike Two and Strike Three. Then when they leave everyone will get a box of Crackerjacks."

Bill taking one last walk around Currie Stadium. It is being demolished this year (2023).

Thanks for the memories ..... The End of an Era....

Bill's Philosophy On Umpiring

Bill Humphrey and myself sat down many times and one time in particular in his wonderful back yard, he opened up about how the national schools began and he paused to collect his thoughts. Bill was appointed to the national umpire staff early in his career and the idea of presenting national schools to all of the ASA umpires was an enormous task, but what foresight.

I didn't tape his talks often but I could tell this was going to be "deep" so I started my phone and recorded it. It was about 8 minutes long and except for a little editing, this is it.

Photo of Bill speaking in back yard.

"We have our first meeting in 77. There was talk with Ron Jeffers, myself and Tom Mason that we should put finally put schools together. I give Tom Mason all the credit in the world because he allowed us to do that and he saw to it that we got it done. That guy is the greatest organizer I've ever known.

I give Tom Mason all the credit in the world because he allowed us to do that. I'm not sure if anything happened on the national level level unless Tom did it. He saw to it that we got it done. Tom knew nothing about schools. He knew nothing about putting a school together.

I know that if it was Ron, and I, you know, I don't know if someone played a more important part than the other, I don't care, that's not what counts because to me it was the three of us that got together we decided to push for this. We brought in Pat Atkinson because he was chairman of the umpire committee that was our way to get to the board and it was Tom Mason who was tenacious as hell when it comes to something he wanted. He knew nothing about it but he wanted to be a part of it.

That's how the national schools happened. Without Tom we can't do anything. Everything we did, we had to go through Tom to get it done, or whatever we thought we should do. I think anything we did under national staff we had to go through Tom.

In the meantime I worked with Tom Mason as a UIC in Midland during the men's major. I think he got a taste of someone who really knew umpire mechanics. I'm just being as honest as I can.

He knew what had been taught in the past but I don't think he really knew mechanics. I've said it before, Tom Mason was the greatest rules man. He would dissect a rule. I think what he learned in working with me and what I learned about looking at rules was how to look at mechanics the way he looked at rules.

Let's break this down for example we had a situation the other day. We got a runner on first base, some guy, a rookie umpire, fast pitch, steal of second base on a passed ball. Who's got third base, that was his question. Rick captured it, "I got third on the play and I'll take that every time." (Rick Havercroft, Saginaw district UIC, was umpiring the Men's Major tournament that weekend in South Bend).

That is not so. That is not ASA. I told Rick, you are wrong. I put it on paper, put it on page, Rick, you're wrong. Do we teach that? No, and there's a reason we don't teach that. Do we approve that? Hell yes we approve that! That's why we teach the system we do, so we can read what the hell's going on. You see that the guy can't make it so I'm covering.

What we don't teach is flip flopping because that's against our one of our basic rules. That talks about keep it simple stupid (KISS method). You can't teach at that time 62,000 umpires. Keep it simple stupid you grow from that. I have said this, Kevin Ryan (national director of umpires) has said this. Kevin Ryan picked it up.

I can't make you a hall of fame umpire. I can't make you an elite umpire. I can teach you the things to get you there but you're the one that's gonna do it. You're the one that's gotta put in the work. you're the one that's gotta be dedicated. You're the one who's gotta want to. I can help and that's what our job is.

I answered Rick on the way to South Bend and good long talk with him about what he's doing I've had it before. First of all Rick is no dummy. I'll tell you that right now, far from it. If you think he's dumb I've got news for you. He's one of the best we have. but I said, you can't answer that as Rick because you are a USA softball Hall of Fame umpire. You can't speak without representing USA so you need to identify that you don't have the title.

I know you're district UIC right now, but I mean when you speak, you're speaking as somebody with all the respect in the world, so you need to speak in terms of USA softball. If you want to know who covers third in the two man system, with a lone runner, it says the base umpire covers the lone runner, the base umpire covers the trail runner, and the base umpire will cover the return throw from the two man system to third base. That's the three things.

Now here's the difference in teaching , why I say what I do when I say put these things together you can put any F****** play you wanna dream up to those three things and apply. you apply (long pause) what do you call, the philosophy to the play not the play to the philosophy. You apply the play to the mechanics not the mechanics to the play.

When I met Tom Mason that was when we developed that philosophy. Did somebody have it before? I don't know. Because I've never heard it, because I've never heard anything presented the way Tom did. there were situations where they had things outlined but they never applied them that way.

You don't know how many times Kevin's called me on a play, wanting to know my feelings. I always go back to that type of thing. Here's what we've got, connect the dots, here's what we got. Then off you go."

LETTER WRITERS

I would include in the book and also present to Bill. I wanted them to say what Bill meant to them and also what he meant to the game of softball.

Four people responded with outstanding letters. They were Kevin Ryan, Gary Evans, and Bryan Smith, all umpires with impressive careers. Debbie Sherwood, assistant to the MASA Director, who worked in the office for over 30 years also responded.

Kevin Ryan: Currently the director of umpires for USA Softball and past umpire in Michigan. Elected to the MASA Hall of Fame in 2005, umpired numerous state, regional, national and world tournaments. He became a member of the state umpire staff in 2002 until being named to the national umpire staff.

Gary Evans: His umpire career began in 1968, served as MASA district umpire-in-chief from 1980-85, later appointed to the state umpire staff and then became the state umpire-in-chief until 2017. Gary umpired in five ASA national slow pitch tournaments. He achieved his National Indicator Fraternity Award in 1984 and the International Softball Federation certification in 1986. Elected to the MASA Hall of Fame in 2014 and the ASA national Hall of Fame in 2016.

Bryan Smith: His umpiring career has taken him from a league umpire to one of the best in the collegiate ranks. Bryan has umpired numerous College World Series games as well as men's major fast pitch tournaments. He was appointed to the MASA state umpire staff in and then to the role of state umpire-in-chief in 2017, a position he still holds.

Debbie Sherwood: Has served as an assistant to the MASA state director for over 30 years. She was hired by Bill Humphrey after he took over for Walt Balcom. She then served for Jerry Hanson when he succeeded Bill and now Darrin Duistermars. A valued person in the state office in Midland, Michigan, her letter has some great insight and humor.

I really don't remember where I met Bill for the first time, all I know he was an imposing figure from his stature and the reputation I had heard about him. What I found out later he was the best thing for the umpire program. He would stand up for the umpires if something wasn't right with uniforms, rules that were not fair for the umpires, or mechanics that didn't make sense. Yes he was a friend for the umpires and he was going to do what was right for the program.

Bill probably left the field earlier than what he wanted to. He had decided it was time for other things to help the game and the umpire program. He accepted a challenge to train and teach umpires. It started with schools and developing an empire manual and manual that is still used today in referred to when clusterings arise. He developed an outline for national schools to get umpires on the same page. He took something that wasn't there and developed the best training manual and guidelines that is the standard for all other softball groups. He literally made the USA softball umpires what they are today.

Years ago while Bill was a commissioner for the state of Michigan, he once again accepted a challenge to try to get things straightened around at the national level. He decided it was time to become president of that time called ASA softball. The commissioners across the country knew that Bill meant business and he cleaned up some things and brought new ideas that are still used today.

For our USA softball of Michigan program, he laid the foundation for others to follow. His knowledge and expertise of not only the umpire program but the game of softball has been so valuable to all of us. Even though, he tries not to get involved as much, he is still looked upon for advice and suggestions and keeping the Michigan program one of the best in the country. He developed a program that other programs across their country tried to copy.

When you say you are from Michigan, people know they have somebody either as an umpire, umpire-in-chief, tournament director, or commissioner that will get the job done. As they know, somehow, Bill Humphrey helped train that individual.

No matter what type of game, umpire, player, commissioner, or umpire-in--chief, when Bill says something about that individual, people listen. He has the most utmost respect across this program from the CEO to the brand new umpire. That respect is earned from what he has done for our program.

We are proud to say that we are from Michigan the home of Bill Humphrey.

Bryan Smith

USA Softball of Michigan, Umpire-in-Chief

I first met Bill Humphrey in the early 1970s. He was umpiring a softball game at Ranney park in Lansing, Michigan. I was a novice umpire who enjoyed softball and wanted to watch some very good softball being umpired by some very good umpires. I was struck immediately by his professional attire, his straight forward approach to the game as he would be the person in charge of the game, his positioning for calling balls, strikes, outs and safes, and the confidence he exuded on the field.

I didn't really meet Bill at those games I observed. Later, I introduced myself to him at umpire clinics he held as the umpire-in-chief for the Michigan Amateur Softball Association. I was hooked. From there it was an umpire development school in Indianapolis in what became the first ASA national umpire school. Bill has the uncanny way of reaching each of the many different people attending this clinics and getting them to feel included in the discussion. That inclusion made it more likely that people would listen and learn about becoming better umpires. Over the years, I learned that his total honesty was the attribute that endeared him most to the people. It was for me! That honesty transcends softball. It is a life lesson.

In evaluating empires or evaluating a job that was given to you, he was honest in telling you his opinion. Most people relish that honesty and their avocation since it was rare in their vocation. If you did a good job, it was acknowledged. If you did a poor job, that was also acknowledged. He puts you in a position to evaluate yourself. That self evaluation made each of us a better umpire and also a better person.

I've used Bill as a sounding board and confident in matters of softball. I saw his expertise and choices I was considering as an umpire on the field and as an umpire staff member. He was always respectful of others opinions on questions of ummpire mechanics and positioning. But he always put priority on what was best for our total organization. I learned to do the same. You cannot have hundreds of conversations during days, nights, and weekends together without life conversations on many other subjects. The characteristics that made bill were exhibits for all of us to learn from.

The respect I have for bill is second only to my family. I realize that desire cannot be taught. But, there are some people in your life that puts you in a frame of mind that encourages that desire to become a reality. I am really thankful that bill Humphrey was one of those people for me.

Always my friend.

Sincerely,

Gary Evans

Past Umpire-In-Chief for Michigan ASA

When I first met Bill Humphrey, the first things that came to mind were that he looks grumpy, gruff, and intimidating. In my mind, I compared him to a Bulldog. Yes, a Bulldog. You know the one in pictures with a big, fat, cigar hanging out of his mouth, and that grumpy face. Yes, Bill can be exactly as I pictured him and described him. But after he hired me to work in the office with him, I soon learned that in addition to those descriptions, Bill is also kind, caring and generous.

Family was important to Bill whether you were his blood family Although softball has been around a little longer than William L. Humphrey, it seems as if the two have been a perfect match. Softball was born in Chicago on Thanksgiving Day, 1887, and Bill was born in Midland on March 18, 1939. Bill was just 13 years old when he began his umpiring career in Midland. As a young boy umpiring local games in Midland, he never imagined that the game of softball, and umpiring, would soon become his passion.

Whether you are in Midland, or Michigan, or even throughout USA and beyond, you can't discuss one without discussing the other. As Bill continued to umpire, it was evident that this was truly a calling. He learned to master his craft, and quickly earned a name for himself in the record books. Not only did he umpire at the local level, soon he was umpiring throughout the state.

Bill's knowledge of the game, mechanics, and control earned him the respect of his fellow umpires. He was appointed as the State Umpire in Chief (UIC) for Michigan, eventually becoming the Regional UIC. His knowledge of the game was second to none. He, along with fellow umpire, Ron Jeffers, began the National Umpire School. Through this school, they held clinics across the country teaching umpires of all levels how to improve their game.

In 1987, with Walt Balcom's retirement, Michigan Amateur Softball Association (MASA) was looking for someone to take over as the Executive Director/Commissioner of Michigan. Bill was the one that the committee chose for this new position. This was a position that Bill held for 13 years. Under his leadership a state office was opened in Midland. MASA was a leader in this as all other ASA associations did not have a full-time office, and staff.

Under Bill's leadership MASA grew and at its highpoint, there were over 6,000 adult teams, and approximately 2,400 umpires registered. Michigan's umpire program is considered one of the best in the country. This is in part due to Bill and his commitment to helping our umpires become the best they could be. Under Bill's leadership, the umpire equipment sales began to help umpires to purchase official gear at clinics.

Bill knew that another area that could help the office with the budget would be to offer softballs for sale. He wanted to offer softballs to our members at more competitive cost than sporting goods stores, but he also made sure that is was profitable for the office. Softball sales continue today.

Bill also had a vision and wanted a Hall of Fame and Museum to showcase those players, umpires, sponsors, commissioners, and those in the meritorious service category. He created the Hall of Fame. There are plaques for each member with a description of their accomplishments. There are numerous memorabilia throughout the Hall of Fame and office.

Again, these are just a few examples where MASA softball, now USA Softball, have benefitted from Bill's love of the game of softball. To say that Bill loves softball is really an understatement. All you have to do is sit with Bill for a few minutes, which eventually turns to hours, to hear stories of long ago. He can tell you the date, time, place, and exactly what the play was.

It is now December of 2022 and although Bill has not been involved with softball on a daily basis for a number of years, there is one thing that comes to mind. You can take Bill out of softball, but you can't take softball out of Bill.

Debbie Sherwood

I have been asked many times in my career who had the most

influence over my umpiring. I would say my true mentor was bill Humphrey. Bill was always a wealth of information about mechanics, rules, and the game. When I say the game, I mean fast, slow and modified. When it came to rules, he helped me understand the written rule, the intent of the rule and the history of the rule. A lot of rules are common with baseball but he taught me in softball some of the rules have a different intent. He taught me to really understand the rules and that I needed to study them.

When it came to mechanics Bill always explained, why we, USA softball, did what we do. He was always available when we had questions and not once did he say, just do what we say. Again, he would explain the whys along with the how to make us better umpires technically but also mentally.

Even though all this was a huge help, the information he shared about the game was what struck me the most. We learned to be a part of the game while not being the game. Hard to do for an umpire and an umpire administrator. He taught me to always remember if they did not play the game we would not be able to do what we do. Be confident but not arrogant, strong in your calls but not just for show and always remember we can be wrong and miss a pitch or a call. The true measure of an umpire is what they do after they missed that pitch or that call. This was huge to me and understanding what makes an umpire.

Bill did not do this just for me, he did this for whoever wanted to listen. He was known for years as the face of USA softball of

Michigan, formerly Michigan ASA. He helped make the umpire program of Michigan known for developing great umpires if one went to a championship anywhere in the country, it was well known they were pretty good umpire. Why, because he would not let you go until you were ready and trained to be one of the best.

He took that drive to help umpires and joined the national umpire staff. He was known for starting the national umpire schools and camps and made sure they were designed to be successful. He personally helped if not wrote, the umpire manual and mechanics that are still used today. He studied the rules and made sure of rules were being introduced as new rules they made sense for the game.

To sum it up when you talk about ASA/USA softball umpires all you have to say is Bill Humphrey. To umpires, a lot of players and coaches, Bill Humphrey was USA softball umpiring.

Kevin C. Ryan

USA Softball Director of Umpires

being interviewed by Midland Daily News

1975 Men's Fast Pitch national umpire crew. Bill Humphrey center back row.

1975 Men's Fast Pitch National tournament umpire crew

Bill Humphrey (kneeling) UIC

Bill in action making a call at the plate.

"You're out!"

"Foul Ball!"

Cleaning the plate

Great plate stance

"strike!"

Page display from "Referee magazine"

Referee magazine edition on greatest officials

National Sports Festival medal

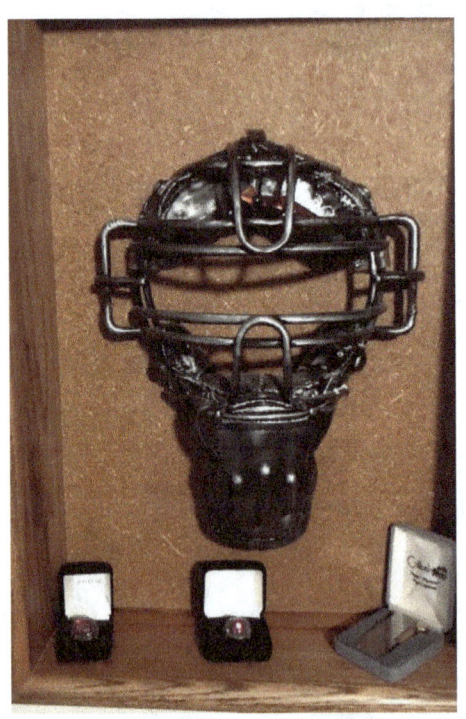

Bill's mask and rings

L to R: Bill Humphrey, David Schimpf, Jerry Hansen

Ron Welch and Bill Humphrey

Bill gestures to Jack Sauder

References

"Softball" – The Barnes Sports Library By Arthur T. Noren. Revised with 1947rules. By A. S. Barnes & Co.

"The Game America Plays" – Celebrating 75 Years of the Amateur Softball Association. By Bill Plummer Copyright 2008. By Arnica Publishing Inc.

"The Evolution and History of Softball in the United States" By Irvin Kawarsky B. S. A field report submitted in Partial Fulfillment of the requirements for The Degree of Master of Science in Education in Drake University. January 1956

"Digital Research Library of Illinois History Journal" Saving Illinois History, One Story at a Time. DRLOIHjournal.blogspot.com

Michigan Amateur Softball History – Prepared by Walt Balcolm, Executive Secretary MASA.1982

Timeline of World War II 1939-1945 – Historic-uk.com and Historic-newspapers.com and thevintagetraveler.wordpress.com and Wikipedia.com

Various tournaments during the mid-1930's – Chicagology.com

Softball – newsletter published in Lansing, Michigan, editor Seth Whitmore

AAGPBL web page

Midland Daily News articles

Balls & Strikes – Official newsletter of ASA

Various newspapers from different cities holding softball tournaments.

www.ingramcontent.com/pod-product-compliance
Lightning Source LLC
Chambersburg PA
CBHW070908120626
46546CB00001B/184